The Will to Power:
The Philosophy
of Friedrich Nietzsche
Part I

Professor Kathleen M. Higgins
Professor Robert C. Solomon

THE TEACHING COMPANY ®

PUBLISHED BY:

THE TEACHING COMPANY
4840 Westfields Boulevard, Suite 500
Chantilly, Virginia 20151-2299
1-800-TEACH-12
Fax—703-378-3819
www.teach12.com

ISBN 1-56585-516-7

Kathleen M. Higgins, Ph.D.

Professor of Philosophy
The University of Texas at Austin

Kathleen Higgins holds the rank of Professor at the University of Texas–Austin. She has a B.A. in Music from the University of Missouri–Kansas City and earned her doctorate in Philosophy (Modern Studies concentration) at Yale University. She has taught at University of California–Riverside and also at the University of Auckland for several summer terms. Among her academic honors are her appointment as Resident Scholar, The Rockefeller Foundation's Bellagio Study and Conference Center and two University Research Institute Awards.

A prolific writer and recognized Nietzsche scholar, her books include *The Music of our Lives* (Temple University Press) and *Nietzsche's* Zarathustra (Temple University Press), which was named one of the Outstanding Academic Books of 1988–1989 by Choice. She has co-edited numerous books with her husband, Professor Robert C. Solomon, including *Reading Nietzsche, A Short History of Philosophy, A Passion for Wisdom, The Philosophy of (Erotic) Love*, and the *Routledge History of Philosophy, Volume IV: The Age of German Idealism*. Additionally, she has authored many articles in scholarly journals, focusing on Nietzsche, but also covering a wide range of other issues in philosophy.

Robert C. Solomon, Ph.D.

Quincy Lee Centennial Professor of Business and Philosophy
The University of Texas at Austin

Robert C. Solomon is Quincy Lee Centennial Professor of Business and Philosophy at the University of Texas at Austin and the recipient of several teaching awards and honors, including the 1973 Standard Oil Outstanding Teaching Award, the University of Texas Presidential Associates' Teaching Award (twice), a Fulbright Lecture Award, University Research and National Endowment for the Humanities Grants and the Chad Oliver Plan Iwe Teaching Award (1998). He is also a member of the Academy of Distinguished Teachers. He is the author of *The Passions* (Doubleday, 1976), *In the Spirit of Hegel, About Love, From Hegel to Existentialism* and *A Passion for Justice*. He has authored and edited articles and books on Nietzsche, including *Nietzsche* and *Reading Nietzsche* with Kathleen M. Higgins. His most recent books, also with Kathleen Higgins, are *A Short History of Philosophy* and *A Passion for Wisdom*. His books have been translated into more than a dozen languages. He also writes about business ethics in *Above the Bottom Line, It's Good Business, Ethics and Excellence*, and *New World of Business* and *A Better Way to Think about Business*. He regularly consults and provides programs for a variety of corporations and organizations concerned about business ethics. He studied Biology at the University of Pennsylvania and Philosophy and Psychology at the University of Michigan. He is married to Kathleen M. Higgins. He has taught at Princeton University, the University of Pittsburgh, and often teaches in New Zealand and Australia.

Table of Contents
The Will to Power:
The Philosophy of Friedrich Nietzsche
Part I

The Will to Power:
The Philosophy of Friedrich Nietzsche

Scope:

Nietzsche is perhaps the best-known and most often quoted philosopher of the last two centuries. He is also probably the most misunderstood, the most misquoted, the most maligned. He is believed to be the Antichrist by some Christians. He is considered power-mad by many pacifists and gentle souls, and by those who themselves are power-mad. He is often thought to have been crazy and it is said to be a tragic irony that sexless Nietzsche died of syphilis. In fact, Nietzsche was deeply religious, that is spiritual, although to be sure he hated the hypocrisy of the Christian church and many of its leaders. (He might better be called an anti-Christian than the Antichrist.) His views on power are complex and much better understood in terms of self-discipline rather than brute force. His sex life is a matter of some debate which we will not delve into, but the diagnosis of the disease that demented and then killed him is by no means straightforward either. The truth is that Nietzsche was and still is the most deeply insightful, personally radical, complex philosopher of modern times.

Nietzsche displayed none of the systematic compulsion of the other great German philosophers, Kant, Fichte and Hegel. Indeed, he argued that the need for a system in philosophy betrayed a "lack of integrity." He shared none of the political radicalism of his near contemporary Karl Marx. Indeed, insofar as Nietzsche pursued any political agenda at all, it might best be described as wishing for a society that appreciated and encouraged creative thinkers like himself. His work is a hodgepodge of reflections, experiments, accusations, bits of psychoanalysis, church and secular history, philosophical counter-examples, advice to the lovelorn, moral reminders, tidbits of gossip, everything but the philosophical kitchen sink. But underlying the hodgepodge is a subtle and intended strategy, and there are profound themes that organize the whole of his work.

In the following lectures, I try to display and work with these themes. Some are well-known but in fact relatively minor threads in his writings. Others are not so well-known and provide the fabric of his thinking. Among the former are certainly his most famous invention, the *Übermensch* and what he calls the Will-to-power. Among the latter are his deep psychological probings that would have such a powerful impact on his successor, Sigmund Freud. Nietzsche specialized in criticism—his attack on Christianity, his repudiation of what is called "morality," his "campaign against guilt and sin," his assault on the modern sensibility, his "critique of Modernity," his personal attacks on his contemporaries and predecessors. But behind all of this is an affirmative fervor, a genuine spirituality, even a religious sensibility. Nietzsche was a lonely man, a self-exile from his German roots who in perpetually poor health depicted a vision of healthy humanity. He was a gentle, extremely polite, thoroughly compassionate man who ruthlessly perceived his own weaknesses and flaws and saw through his own pretensions and virtues. Like Socrates who proclaimed his own ignorance and used this as a platform to expose the ignorance of everyone else around him, Nietzsche begins by insisting on his own "self-overcoming" and challenges us to do the same. But even at his most brutal and most provocative, Nietzsche exudes an enthusiasm, and a love of life that is really the heart of his philosophy. To love and accept one's life, to make it better by becoming who one really is, that is what Nietzsche's philosophy is ultimately all about.

In the first of these twenty-four lectures, We begin by describing, very briefly, Nietzsche's rather unremarkable life and the rather more remarkable times in which he lived. He was born just a few years before the tumultuous revolutions of mid-century (1844), and he died in the first summer of what he predicted would be a new and most violent century. I then describe, also briefly, the sequence of works that has come down to us, also noting the suspicious forgeries of his works by his nefarious sister. We then begin to unfold the grand themes of his philosophy. In the second lecture, I discuss (with the help of my wife, fellow Nietzsche scholar Kathleen Higgins), various "rumors" about Nietzsche, beginning with the rumor that he was crazy and rumors about his sex life. We then move into some of the more subtle misunderstandings about his attitudes toward religion in general, toward Christianity in particular, toward the Jews, toward German nationalism and patriotism, and his complex relationship with the great operatic composer Richard Wagner. In the third lecture, we discuss Nietzsche's fusion of philosophy and psychology and relate this back to some of the great figures in philosophy, notably Socrates and Schopenhauer, Plato, and Jesus.

We also discuss the uncanny connection between anti-Christian Nietzsche and the Danish philosopher Søren Kierkegaard, a Christian fundamentalist whom Nietzsche never had the chance to read. Comparisons with Dostoevsky, Marx and Freud are also mentioned.

The next several lectures concern Nietzsche's famous announcement that "God is Dead." We try to explain what this means—it is by no means merely a thesis about religion and religious belief, and how it relates to the larger themes of Nietzsche's philosophy. We discuss Nietzsche's Lutheranism, his rejection of it and also the way that it continues to influence his thinking. We discuss in what sense Nietzsche is a champion of spirituality, and in what senses he is not. In the fifth lecture, we discuss Nietzsche's intimate relation with the ancient Greeks. Indeed, Nietzsche's love of philology and his near-worship of ancient Greeks has been argued to be the underlying motive if not also the theme of his whole philosophy. But Nietzsche is not the only German who displayed what one author has called "the tyranny of Greece over Germany." Nietzsche's relation to the ancient Greeks was complex, however. He loved the ancient tragic playwrights Aeschulus and Sophocles, but he despised their younger colleague Euripides. He displayed great admiration for the pre-Socratic philosopher Heraclitus but had evident contempt for the great philosophers Socrates and Plato. But even his contempt was complex and mixed. It is obvious that he envied Socrates even as he ridiculed him. Socrates, along with Jesus, was something of a role model for Nietzsche. Indeed, not only Socrates' success but his reputation for virtue was something that Nietzsche admired. Nevertheless, the very heart of Socrates' (and Plato's) philosophy, the celebration of reason, was one of Nietzsche's primary targets for abuse. In the sixth lecture, we discuss in more detail Nietzsche's conception of tragedy, and along with it his conception of comedy, comparing the former with his predecessors Aristotle, Hegel and Schopenhauer. We introduce Nietzsche's famous opposition between the Apollonian and Dionysian aspects of Greek culture, and we discuss the sense in which the Greeks "accepted" suffering and made something "beautiful" out of it. The contrast, for Nietzsche, is with Christianity, which tries to deny the meaning of suffering by way of the invocation of another, better "otherwordly" life. (So, too, Nietzsche says, did Socrates and Plato.)

In the seventh lecture, we provide arguments for and against pessimism, with an emphasis on Nietzsche's early hero,

Schopenhauer. We discuss Nietzsche's efforts to embrace "cheerfulness," if not optimism, and his discussion of the aesthetic viewpoint, of life as art. We also discuss the role of reason and passion in the meaning of life. In the eighth lecture, we discuss Nietzsche's emphasis on instinct, his debunking of reason and consciousness, his notion of reason as a tyrant, his insights into the nature of passion. In the ninth lecture, we discuss Nietzsche's style, his use of "*ad hominem* arguments" and other informal fallacies, such as his appeal to emotion. We then move into Nietzsche's often exaggerated views about truth and interpretation. In the tenth lecture, we discuss in more detail Nietzsche's views on these matters and his "perspectivism," his idea that there is no privileged, objective, absolute, or "God's eye" view of the world or human affairs.

In the eleventh lecture, we discuss in more detail Nietzsche's intimate and envious relation to the prophets of old, Jesus, Socrates and the Persian sage Zoroaster or Zarathustra. We discuss Nietzsche's oddest but best known book, *Thus Spoke Zarathustra*, a Biblical parody in which the Persian prophet rejects Christianity and all "otherworldly" ways of living and introduces the idea of the *Übermensch*. He also introduces the supposedly hateful idea of "the last man," the probable successor of modern man, the ultimate *bourgeois*, the perfectly happy couch potato. In the twelfth lecture, we discuss Nietzsche's politics (such as they were), his individualism, his harsh views on socialism and democracy, his notorious views on "the great man." Accordingly, we also discuss Nietzsche's mixed reviews of Darwin's theory of evolution, which he clearly embraced in general outline even as he quibbled violently with the details. We also discuss his relation to Hegel, an important predecessor whom he evidently knew only by reputation. Hegel is often said to have anticipated Darwin (a debatable claim), but he clearly both anticipated and countered some of Nietzsche's main concerns. (In their reaction to Hegel, Nietzsche and Kierkegaard show themselves to be particularly kindred spirits.) We also discuss Nietzsche's subtle views on freedom and free will, his celebration of fate (*amor fati*) and his insistence that one should "become who [you] are."

In the thirteenth lecture, we discuss in much more detail Nietzsche as a philosophical psychologist and his many insights and provocations concerning such basic human emotions as pity (compassion) and love. We discuss more generally Nietzsche's "moral psychology" and how it provides a counter to the more traditional philosophical attempts to justify (rather than explain) morality. In the fourteenth lecture, we discuss in more detail Nietzsche's views (and experiences) about love.

In the fifteenth lecture, we run through a dozen or so of Nietzsche's *ad hominem* analyses and attacks on various figures, first discussing those figures whom he (more or less) admires, and then those whom he (more and even more) despises. In effect, we (with Kathleen) produce two "top (and bottom) ten" lists, Nietzsche's favorites and Nietzsche's targets. In the sixteenth lecture, we discuss the grounds on which he makes such harsh evaluations, discussing Nietzsche's view of the use and abuse of history, his hopes for human evolution, his pervasive concern with what is healthy and what is "sickly," his celebration of *life*. In the seventeenth lecture, we discuss his views on nihilism, making the point that Nietzsche himself was no nihilist. Indeed, nihilism might well be described as the most general target of his entire philosophy.

In the eighteenth lecture, we discuss Nietzsche's ranking of values, his view of morality and moralities, and his critique of modernity. In the nineteenth lecture, we discuss Nietzsche's "immoralism" and the senses in which he both was and was not a moralist. We argue that Nietzsche is embracing an ancient rather than a modern view of ethics, what has been called an "ethics of virtue" rather than an ethics of rules and principles, rather than an ethic that looks mainly to the spread of well-being and happiness ("utilitarianism"). In the twentieth lecture, we discuss Nietzsche's polemic on weakness, his archaeological history ("genealogy") of morality, and his analysis of master and slave (or "herd") morality. In the twenty-first lecture, we discuss master and slave morality in more detail and analyze Nietzsche's notion of *ressentiment* that provides the basis of his moral psychology. In the next lecture, we discuss Nietzsche's analysis of resentment, revenge, and justice, and we follow this with a diagnosis of asceticism, the thorough-going self-denial that is often an extreme form of religious practices. In the twenty-third and twenty-fourth lectures, we discuss three of Nietzsche's most famous doctrines, the Will to Power, the *Übermensch*, and eternal recurrence, and we end by evaluating Nietzsche's emphasis on saying *"Yes!"* to *Life* and at the same time "philosophizing with a hammer."

Lecture One
Why Read Nietzsche?
His Life, Times, Works, and Themes

Scope:

Nietzsche is, perhaps, the most exciting philosopher—ever! Not just because he is so obviously smart. Not just because he writes so beautifully. Not just because of all the enthusiasm and exclamation points. Not even just because of his peculiar ideas and themes and topics. But because Nietzsche forces us to think and rethink, more than anyone else in the modern Western tradition. He provokes us. He teases us. He seduces us. Nietzsche changes lives (true, in the case of young students, often in transient, mildly delusional ways). But for others, he offers nothing less than new life. And it is this lonely, frantic, self-styled prophet who flips the switch into the tumultuous, horrendous twentieth century.

In this lecture, we begin by describing, very briefly, Nietzsche's rather unremarkable life and the rather more remarkable times in which he lived. The times included the rise of Bismarck and the unification of Germany, a short but dramatic war (in which Nietzsche briefly served), some remarkable advances in science and news ways of thinking about art and culture. Nietzsche's life, for the most part, was lived through and defined by his writing. He was a brilliant student who became a brilliant young professor. He became ill soon after the Franco-Prussian War, spent most of his adult life "wandering" between the most beautiful mountain towns and resorts in Southern Europe, writing and thinking ferociously and, for the most part, alone. He proposed marriage twice, but was turned down, as he must have known that he would be.

Outline

I.   To make sense of Nietzsche, we present a quick tour of his major ideas; these will be developed more fully in the subsequent twenty-three lectures:

   A. *Übermensch*

   B. Nihilism

   C. Will-to-power

D. Apollonian and Dionysian

E. The Attack on Christianity

F. The Repudiation of Morality

G. The War against Guilt and Sin

H. The Love of Fate (*Amor Fati*) and of Living Dangerously

I. The Critique of Modernity

J. Saying "Yes!" to Life

K. The Eternal Recurrence

II. Nietzsche's life (1844–1900) was short and, in the heroic sense, uneventful.

    A. During Nietzsche's life, Otto von Bismarck took control first of Prussia and then of a united Germany. Germany defeated France in the Franco-Prussian War of 1870–1871.

        1. Nietzsche participated as a medical orderly. He became seriously ill during this time.

        2. Although a very gentle person, he never lost his fascination for and admiration of the discipline of the military.

    B. Nietzsche's productive life was very short. He spent most of his adult life, from his teaching in Switzerland to his final collapse in Italy, outside Germany (in some of the most beautiful places in Europe).

    C. For many people, Nietzsche's mustache is his defining physical feature.

        1. His mustache represented military discipline for him.

        2. It served him as a mask; it allowed him to hide.

    D. Nietzsche fell in love with (and was rejected by) Lou Salomé during 1882, when he was beginning sketches for *Thus Spoke Zarathustra*; he began to suffer serious bouts of depressions.

    E. As a young professor, Nietzsche met and befriended composer Richard Wagner and his wife, Cosima.

        1. For several years, Nietzsche was a worshipful and sometimes fawning follower.

        2. When the friendship ended a few years later, Nietzsche was devastated and alone.

3. Nietzsche cut off relations with his sister Elizabeth after she married a proto-Nazi.
4. Nietzsche collapsed in Turin in January of 1889 and spent the rest of his life hopelessly insane.

III. Nietzsche's work passes through several indistinct stages.

    A. First, there is the heavily classical emphasis in the Greeks, culminating in *The Birth of Tragedy* (1872).

    B. *The Untimely Meditations* follow:
        1. One was on a contemporary historian who considered the life of Jesus historically.
        2. The second was on historical knowledge and its value for the present era.
        3. The third was on Schopenhauer as Nietzsche's educator.
        4. The third was a paean to Richard Wagner, which appeared as their friendship was nearing its end.

    C. Nietzsche's aphoristic style dominates the experimental works: *Human, All Too Human* (1878), *Daybreak* (1881), and *The Gay (Fröliche) Science* (1882). In these works, Nietzsche begins his "campaign against morality."

    D. His quasi-biblical epic poem, *Thus Spoke Zarathustra*, was written in several outbursts and published in parts from 1883 through 1885; Zarathustra became Nietzsche's alter ego and spokesperson.

    E. In *Beyond Good and Evil* (1886) and *On the Genealogy of Morals* (1887), Nietzsche became more systematic.

    F. In his last active year, 1888, Nietzsche miraculously produced four books: *The Wagner Case*, *Twilight of the Idols*, *The Antichrist*, and an autobiography, *Ecce Homo*.

Essential Reading:

R. J. Hollingdale, ed., *A Nietzsche Reader*, Preface, pp. 15–25, *Ecce Homo*, "Why I am so Wise," "Why I am so Clever."

Supplemental Reading:

Bernd Magnus and Kathleen M. Higgins, "Introduction to Nietzsche's Works" in *Cambridge Companion*, pp. 21–68.

R. J. Hollingdale, "The Hero as Outsider" in *Cambridge Companion*, pp. 71–89. Three full-length biographies: Ronald Hayman, *Nietzsche* (an excellent biography); David Farrel Krell, *The Good European* (a stunning collection of photographs and letters); Leslie Chamberlain, *Nietzsche in Turin* (a moving account of Nietzsche's last years).

A Note on the Recommended Reading:

Nietzsche was not a systematic philosopher and did not (in general) divide or subdivide his books into distinct topics or themes. For this reason, the recommended reading will consist mostly of fragments. For convenience (and expense), we have made recommendations from several sources, including collections and books of selections. So, too, in the Supplemental Reading, we have sometimes referred the reader to collections of essays (on Nietzsche) as well as to whole books on a topic. (Publication details are in the bibliography.)

Recommended Reading:

R. J. Hollingdale, ed., *A Nietzsche Reader*.

Walter Kaufmann, ed., *Basic Writings of Nietzsche*.

————, ed., *The Portable Nietzsche*.

Richard Schacht, ed., *Nietzsche: Selections*.

(We have not given page numbers for any of Nietzsche's full works, because editions and translations vary.)

Supplemental Reading:

Kathleen M. Higgins, *Nietzsche's* Zarathustra.

Bernd Magnus and Kathleen M. Higgins, *Cambridge Companion to Nietzsche*.

Richard Schacht, ed., *Nietzsche: Selections* and *Genealogy, Morality*.

Robert C. Solomon, ed., *Nietzsche: A Collection of Critical Essays*.

———— and Kathleen M. Higgins, eds., *Reading Nietzsche*.

———— and Kathleen M. Higgins, *What Nietzsche Really Said*.

Additional Recommended Original Work in Full:

Gay Science, Daybreak.

Questions to Consider:

1. Could a thinker like Nietzsche have appeared anytime earlier in Western philosophy? Could someone like Nietzsche appear with similar impact today?

2. Is it possible to be a moral person even while declaring oneself an atheist, an "immoralist," an *Antichrist*? What is the connection (if any) between a person's beliefs and his or her moral character?

Lecture One—Transcript
Why Read Nietzsche?
His Life, Times, Works, and Themes

Hi. I'm Bob Solomon. I want to begin with a confession: I am in love with Nietzsche. I have been since I started reading him in high school. Since then, I have read him I don't know how many times; I've written books, articles; and I married a fellow Nietzsche scholar, whom you'll meet shortly. Nietzsche fascinates me. He always seduces me. At the same time, he is outrageous, he is infuriating, he is inconsistent, and I always find myself trying to make sense of it even after thirty years.

What I would like to do in these lectures is to try to give some system, some shape, to Nietzsche's thought, and I want to be very clear that I am not going to try to formalize him or even systematize him as much as run through some of his most famous themes. Some of them, no doubt, will offend you, too. That's intentional. Nietzsche wanted to be polemical; his whole philosophy is aimed not at presenting a worldview so much as making us think and, in particular, making us examine ourselves and ultimately love our lives. The themes are famous enough, and these lectures will be structured around them.

First of all, of course, there is the infamous doctrine of the Übermensch, the superman, an almost cartoon-like character that, in fact, plays a very small role in Nietzsche's actual writing and is made famous more by George Bernard Shaw, who wrote a parodic play of him, than by the real centrality in Nietzsche's philosophy. Nevertheless, it's an important doctrine, and it helps us to understand some of the ways that Nietzsche was thinking. There is the equally infamous notion of the "will to power," which sounds as ominous as can be, especially given German history of the last hundred years or so. In fact, it's much more benign than it sounds and has much more to do with personal self-discipline and strength than it does with anything like military might.

Nietzsche talks in his first work and then throughout his career about the twin Greek deities Apollo and Dionysus. In his first work, he talks about the Apollonian, which is the individual, the rational, and about the Dionysian, which is the sort of frenzied orgiastic sense in which we feel ourselves as part of life flowing through us, and, of course, that's going to be an important image throughout Nietzsche's philosophy.

There is his attack on Christianity. When I made a trip to give a lecture in North Texas just couple of months ago, I was informed very somberly over dinner that Nietzsche was the Antichrist. That's not quite fair, but perhaps one could say he is anti-Christian, or, at least, he is certainly anti the kind of Christianity that he saw around him. But, as we are going to argue, there is a good deal of Christianity, a good deal of Lutheranism that remains in his philosophy, and Nietzsche is anything but a philosopher who is against the notion of spirituality.

We are going to talk about nihilism, which is a very current word. Nietzsche has often been accused of being a nihilist, namely, a philosopher who believes in nothing, who does nothing but destroy. What I would like to show is that the exact opposite is true, that what Nietzsche attacks are mainly values that he considers both popular and nihilistic, values that ultimately, as he puts it, devalue themselves. I also want to talk about his famous repudiation of morality. Nietzsche sometimes calls himself an immoralist. Well, yes and no. He certainly is a man who lived a perfectly respectable life. Everyone who knew him would comment on his courtesy, his generosity, his niceness, but, nevertheless, what he says about morality is often very harsh, and what I would like to argue is that what Nietzsche tries to do is to get us to think about morals, about ethics, about values in a different way.

Part of the campaign against Christianity, against morality, is what Nietzsche calls his war against guilt and sin. Of course, he is not the only one. A few years later, Freud was to undertake a similar campaign. Guilt is neurotic; guilt is not good for you. Guilt is not simply taking responsibility for your actions, but it is putting a metaphysical weight on them that they don't deserve. We are going to talk about Nietzsche's fatalism, his love of fate, what he calls "amor fati." It's the idea that we have a destiny, the idea that we are born with talents and potentials. The idea of his philosophy, in many ways, is to get us to become who we are, as he puts it, a phrase he borrows again from ancient Greece. And along with this there is the notion of living dangerously, a phrase that is often repeated, particularly by my undergraduates, but in fact, what he means is taking risks—for example, taking risks in what you say and what you think, not just following the herd. And Nietzsche, of course, is perhaps the best living example of that kind of an attitude.

When you are talking about a single philosopher or a single thinker, of course, it's very important to talk about the biography. Who was this guy? In particular, in Nietzsche's case, Nietzsche taught that the philosopher should be an example, and he made enormous demands of the philosophers of the past—Socrates, for example, or Immanuel Kant—to sort of live through their philosophy and would always ask the question, "What does the philosophy say about the philosopher?" And, the other way around, "What does the philosopher show us about the philosophy?" Well, of course, having said that, it becomes imperative as well as fair to apply the same thesis to Nietzsche himself, and so the question is, "What kind of a man was this who presented us with such images as the Übermensch, the will to power, and the Apollonian and Dionysian; who attacked Christianity and morality right at its very roots; who attacked modern life as being decadent; who talked about fatalism; who talked about living dangerously?"

The story can be told, in a way, very briefly. Nietzsche had a very unhappy life. He did not live all that long. As almost everyone knows, he died after ten years of nearly total insanity. His productive years were, in fact, very short. He wrote his first book in 1872 and his last books in 1888. In between, he had a really miraculous production of some of the best German prose and some of the wildest and most interesting German thinking that's to be found in the entire culture or, for that matter, in all of Europe.

Talking about Nietzsche's life, let's start with the obvious, and that is with Nietzsche's mustache. Nietzsche had a mustache for most of his mature life. In the pictures we have of him when he was a young professor in Switzerland, he already is sporting a mighty handsome upper lip. Of course, one of the most famous depictions of him, a photograph taken very late in life when he was already insane, is a very wild, rich mustache that most of us probably couldn't wear in public. Unfortunately, that's often taken as *the* depiction of Nietzsche. It's unfair. The twinkle in his eye is gone; it's replaced by the gaze of someone who has literally lost his mind. Nevertheless, the mustache is something that he lived with most of his adult life and he sometimes talked about.

In particular, the mustache for him represented the military life. Nietzsche, in fact, served in the military only very briefly, and I will talk about that in a moment, but, basically, he never lost a certain kind of fascination, a certain sort of admiration, for military discipline. That's not to say that he was a warmonger or, for that matter, liked war at all, approved of it—no. But what we get in Nietzsche is always this sense that the military attitude is very important towards living a proper, fulfilling life, and, although a mustache might not look as if it represents discipline, in Nietzsche's mind, that is certainly part of the picture.

The other part, perhaps, is more telling. Nietzsche said in several different places that the mustache was a kind of a mask. After all, if you ask most people, "What does Nietzsche look like?" what they will immediately say is, "Oh, that's the guy with the huge moustache," and if you ask, "Well, what about the eyes, what about the nose, what about the chin, what about the hair?" they will probably draw a blank. And Nietzsche himself points out that when you see someone with a big, handsome mustache, what they see is the mustache; it is a mask. It allowed Nietzsche, in effect, to hide. The underlying psychological truth of Nietzsche's life, and certainly his mature life, was that he was alone. I want to talk about that in a little bit of detail, but first let's go back to the beginning.

He was born in a small, German town in 1844. He was raised as a Lutheran. In fact, his father was a Lutheran minister; his mother, his aunts, and his grandmother were all pious Lutherans. His father, sadly, died when he was only four years old, so he was raised in a family of women, in a family of pious Lutherans, and, of course you don't have to be a deep Freudian to think this is what he is reacting against later in his comments about Christianity but perhaps more infamously in some of his often-quoted comments about women. He grew up as obviously a very bright young man, and early in life he fell in love.

What he fell in love with were the classics, and that, of course, was the career that he then pursued. He proved himself a very able student. He got a professorship at the unbelievable age of twenty-four years old and had a brilliant career in front of him. Unfortunately, before that career progressed very far, he served in the Franco-Prussian War of 1870-71 as a medical orderly. Even so, he had already given up his German citizenship, and he was, in fact, a Swiss citizen throughout his career. I was told at dinner just a few nights ago by a young man that Nietzsche was, together with Rousseau, one of the great Swiss philosophers of all time.

It's very tongue in cheek, but it's an important point since Nietzsche is so often affiliated with German, German military thinking, and so on. It's important to point out that, in fact, he lived most of his mature life in Switzerland and in northern Italy and not in Germany. When he was in the military for a brief time, he contracted some series of diseases, and many of them progressed over the years to the point where, by the late 1870s, he had to resign the professorship. He spent the rest of his life, in fact, wandering, for the most part alone, in some of the most gorgeous spots in the world. He spent time in a small town called Sils-Maria, he spent time in Nice, and he spent a good deal of time in various places around the Alps, the lakes in northern Italy, and in southern Switzerland.

He was a man with a keen aesthetic eye, and it's very clear that in his loneliness what he really wanted was beauty that would make him feel more alive, make him feel more at home on earth, give him something to look at, be a good place to think. But it is hard to underestimate the loneliness. Early in his life, he had proposed to a young woman after a courtship of what today we would call maybe a date and a half. Not too surprisingly, he was turned down.

More dramatically, in 1882, while he was writing what became one of his most famous books, *Thus Spoke Zarathustra,* he met a woman who, in retrospect as well as at the time, was certainly one of the most dazzling women in Europe—both intellectually, in terms of personality, and in terms of looks. Lou Salomé was a beautiful young woman who, in fact, later on would write one of the first insider books on Nietzsche. She was also a friend of Rilke and later would become a friend of Freud. She played a pivotal role in German European intellectual life. Nietzsche fell madly in love with her and spent quite a few months with her, but, again, when he tried to change from friendship to romance, when he proposed, he was turned down, and he virtually never got over it.

Earlier in life, he had befriended the composer Richard Wagner, and that friendship was very close for several years, but that, too, ended in disappointment, and again Nietzsche says, "I never felt so alone." In fact, here is a quote that comes from about 1884, a few years after both of these situations: "Almost all of my human relations have resulted from attacks of a feeling of isolation. I have not been so profoundly ill for nothing, and I am ill on the average now still, that is to say, depressed, simply because I was lacking the right milieu and always had to playact somewhat instead of refreshing myself in people. I do not for that reason consider myself secret or furtive or a mistrustful person. Quite the reverse—if I was that, I would not suffer so much."

That was his letter to his sister, who would play another important role in his life. They were close as children, but, in 1884, in fact, just at the time this letter was written, his sister married a man whom Nietzsche utterly despised, and the reason for that, I think, is something very important. Elizabeth's husband-to-be and husband was what we would call a proto-Nazi. He was a fascist in temperament, and he was an anti-Semite, and Nietzsche found these views so despicable that he virtually cut off relations with his sister, with whom he was very friendly, and that relationship would not be fully renewed until Nietzsche collapsed and essentially was completely helpless, at which point his sister helped first to take care of him and, more problematically, took over his literary estate. In fact, some of the books that we have from Nietzsche that are no longer at all respectable were edited and perhaps even in part written by his sister Elizabeth.

The collapse itself came in 1889. Nietzsche was in Turin in northern Italy. Again, the circumstances are telling. He embraced a horse who was been beaten by its owner—clearly an act of intense compassion, not to mention a kind of sense of animal rights. When he did so, he collapsed. He was never the same again. His friends came, got him, and took him eventually back to Germany, where he was cared for by his mother until she died and then by his sister until he died. It's a very sad story. So it's a story of a lonely man who at the same time had incredible genius. Let me raise a question that will come up later: What do we make of works that are so bold and courageous coming from a man whose life was basically miserable? I think one way to look at it, of course, is to say the works, the ideas were compensation for the life. I think there is a better way, and the better way is to say the works were Nietzsche's life.

Lets talk about those works. In 1872, Nietzsche wrote his first book, *The Birth of Tragedy*. It was without footnotes; it was outrageous; it was not the book that his academic colleagues had expected. It defended the thesis that tragedy arose among the Greeks out of a combination of two forces: Apollonian, the individual, the rationalistic represented, for example, by Socrates, and then the Dionysian derived from the Orphic cults. It was orgiastic. It is that sense of life flowing together and the brilliance of the Greeks.

The way the Greeks invented tragedy, but, more importantly, the way the Greeks learned to cope with a very difficult life was by combining these two forces and understanding that life was tragic. It's a sense we have lost now, and a good deal of the book is the comparison between the Greeks and ourselves. In fact, much of Nietzsche's career and a good deal of German philosophy in the nineteenth century could be characterized in terms of a profound admiration, even an envy, for the way ancient Greeks lived—their sense of life, their sense of vitality—and the contrast is with what is now called modernity and a life that is defined by middle-class or bourgeois values.

In the following year, 1873, Nietzsche begins a series of what was intended to be thirteen essays called *Untimely* or *Unfashionable Meditations*. The first of these was a meditation on the life of Jesus. More directly, it was a meditation on a contemporary writer on the life of Jesus. In a way, it's a nasty piece of work, nasty, that is, towards the contemporary writer. Towards Jesus, however, it wasn't really nasty at all. In fact, a point to be made given Nietzsche's reputation as a harsh anti-Christian is that, where Jesus is concerned, Nietzsche pretty much leaves him alone and, in fact, often expresses a kind of admiration, if not so much for his teachings then certainly for him as a man.

The second meditation was a meditation on history and, given Nietzsche's admiration, almost worship, of the ancient Greeks, it provides a very important counterbalance because there is a danger that Nietzsche sees very clearly in his profession of philology in particular but in intellectual life in Germany in general: that the admiration for the ancients could be so great that it would be overwhelming, that one would simply dismiss contemporary life and spend all the time just wallowing in history and wallowing in the classics. The theme of the second essay is, basically, that we should use history and we should use history in particular to make our lives better and richer.

The third essay is about one of the Nietzsche's most profound influences, the German philosopher Arthur Schopenhauer. Schopenhauer is widely known as the great pessimist or, perhaps we could say, the great crank in philosophical history. His sense was, in a word, that life is no good. Schopenhauer had a magnificent philosophy to back this up—he is one of the most brilliant of German writers—but Nietzsche never accepted the pessimism, although he was greatly in awe of what Schopenhauer had done as a philosopher. In fact, one could look at Nietzsche's whole career as an attempt to slough off Schopenhauer's pessimism and maintain instead, in line with the ancient Greeks, that life is good, life is great. In fact, even if it contains suffering, even if it involves tragedy, even if it ends in death, nevertheless, life is something to be enjoyed. Life is something to be profoundly felt.

The fourth essay is an essay on another of the great influences on Nietzsche's life, and that's the composer Wagner. It is very much an admiring essay, and there is an irony to this because it was published just at the time when, in fact, the relationship between Nietzsche and Wagner was disintegrating. And perhaps it's worth saying that the most important point of disagreement between them, where Nietzsche really threw off Wagner entirely, was because of Wagner's anti-Semitism. Nietzsche is often listed as a kind of proto-Nazi, as an anti-Semite, and this is one of several times when it becomes absolutely crystal clear that one of the dominant themes of Nietzsche's life was a kind of anti anti-Semitism.

In 1878, Nietzsche begins a remarkable series of books; it's when Nietzsche really becomes Nietzsche. The first consists of a several-volume set called *Human, All Too Human*, and what is immediately striking about these books and the couple of books to follow is they are written in aphorisms—very short, often one-line or at least one-short- paragraph bits—which have some profound insight, some great exclamation, some probing question, some historical anecdote, but the basic idea, as in all of Nietzsche's works, is to jar us, to make us think about things in a different way, to get us to see things in different perspectives.

The second of this series is a book called *Daybreak*, indicating a kind of new dawn in Nietzsche's philosophy. It begins what he calls his campaign against morality and, in effect, what it does is it looks at a good many of our moral prejudices, it looks at a good deal of our moral ideals, and what it points out is that, behind the facade of the divine given commandment, behind the facade of the rational principle, often is a kind of dirty, little secret, a bit of selfishness, a bit of smugness, a bit of superiority. For example, regarding the emotion of pity or compassion, which almost all authors have praised back to the ancient Chinese, but also Kant and Schopenhauer, Nietzsche points out that very often our pity is really nothing but a kind of superiority.

Following *Daybreak*, Nietzsche publishes what is probably his most personal book, a book called *The Gay Science*. It is also largely aphoristic. In it, he introduces such themes as the death of God and the extremely life-affirming thesis that he calls eternal recurrence, the idea that we live our lives not just once but over and over and over again. This is a thesis that is not supposed to depress us; to the contrary, it's supposed to give us great joy. After this, Nietzsche publishes two books on ethics. The first, *Beyond Good and Evil*, summarizes much of his philosophy to date. It includes meditations on philosophy in general in which he says, for example, that every philosophy is really the work of confession. It's an unconscious memoir. It is not, as philosophers present it, simply a set of abstract ideas.

The next book, *Genealogy of Morals*, expands on one thesis from *Beyond Good and Evil* in particular. It's the idea that there are two kinds of morality, not just one. There is master morality, which is, as this term indicates, the morality of the aristocrats, the morality of the warriors, the morality of the heroes of ancient Greece, and then there is slave morality, a morality that comes from oppression, from servile conditions, from weakness, from inferiority. He goes on to say that what we call morality is really just slave morality. It's a very polemical thesis, and Nietzsche announces it as such. It is often offensive, but it's an offense with a point, and, again, the point is to get us to think about morality, which we often praise unthinkingly in a different way.

In his last active year, Nietzsche goes ahead and publishes four books. The first of them is called *Twilight of The Idols*. It is, in my mind, one of Nietzsche's greatest books. It includes a protracted attack on Socrates, it attacks reason, it attacks morality as being something that is unnatural, it talks about the prejudices and mistakes in the tradition of philosophy going back to Aristotle, and it includes a long section that he calls "The Skirmishes of an Untimely Man," in which he, among other things, attacks many of his contemporaries, especially some folks who seem rather close to him in ideas. We will be talking about that, too.

He also publishes a book on Wagner. In this case, it's no longer praise, no longer anything like the worshipful or even admiring stance that he had taken in the early essay. Now it's Wagner as combining everything wrong with contemporary society. He also publishes *The Antichrist*—the title itself is enough to tell us this is a conscientiously polemical book—and an autobiography, *Ecce Homo*. Finally, there is a book called *The Will to Power*. This, of course, is a phrase Nietzsche often used. I have much to say about it, but the book itself really is not a book at all. It's a book of notes, a book of jottings, that was put together first by Nietzsche's sister Elizabeth and then reedited several times.

But the important point about it is Nietzsche didn't write it. He may have written the notes, but I know my office is filled with notes, observations, insights, ideas for books, ideas for titles, and much of it's written on napkins, scraps of paper, and so on. I will never get it together. But it would horrify me to think that someone might get it together and publish it as something of mine because there is a reason why those things are not published. It's because I didn't think they were polished enough or, in some cases, I just didn't have a chance to throw them away. Many times it's just wackiness that I kind of enjoyed sticking out there, but I wouldn't ever put my name to it in public, and that's the way I want to read that particular book of Nietzsche's, too. Not that it doesn't contain some wonderful quotes—Nietzsche was a brilliant stylist and had a wonderful turn of phrase and so on—but I think the important point is that, with Nietzsche, trust the published works. If something in the unpublished works matches up, then it's a different way of saying the same thing. That's fine.

In the following lectures, I am not going to be going through Nietzsche book by book, although that is certainly one way to approach it, but rather in terms of themes, and what I am going to be after, to be very brief about it, is to try and make you fall in love with Nietzsche, too.

Lecture Two
Quashing the Rumors about Nietzsche

Scope:

In this lecture, we discuss (with the help of my wife, fellow Nietzsche scholar Kathleen Higgins), some of the malicious and misplaced "rumors" about Nietzsche that have come down to us through the years. In particular, we want to quash the charge that Nietzsche was crazy and so not to be taken seriously as a philosopher and the often vicious personal charges: that he hated women; that he was a Nazi; an anti-Semite and a nihilist who believed that "everything is permitted"; that he condoned war, murder and cruelty; that he had no sex life, yet died of syphilis. We also want to set aside the ways in which Nietzsche did and did not hate Christianity and religion in general. Philosophically, his thought should also be carefully distinguished with such "red-flag" doctrines as egoism and relativism. We briefly take up the issues surrounding Nietzsche's unorthodox and controversial style.

Outline

I. The rumors and responses to them are as follows:

   A. Nietzsche was crazy.

      1. Nietzsche was mentally ill during the last twelve years of his life.

      2. His writings do not support the speculation that he was already mad during his creative period.

   B. Nietzsche had syphilis.

      1. Nietzsche was diagnosed with syphilis in the asylum in Jena in 1889.

      2. Interest in the source of this disease is disappointed by Nietzsche's discretion about his sex life.

   C. Nietzsche had no sex life.

      1. It has recently been suggested that Nietzsche was gay, with some evidence.

      2. Again, Nietzsche's discretion disappoints interests in his sex life.

D. Nietzsche was hostile toward women.
1. He grew up in a household of women.
2. He was aware of the influence of family relationships (particularly his relationship with his mother) on his attitude toward women.
3. Nietzsche rejected the aims of the contemporary feminist movement.
4. Nietzsche opposed the uni-sex, one-size-fits-all ideal.

E. Nietzsche was hostile toward Christians.
1. Nietzsche disliked some things about Christianity, particularly what Kierkegaard calls "Christendom," the Christian mob.
2. Nietzsche admired those exceptional Christians (including Jesus) who really lived what they claimed to believe in.
3. He objected to the hypocritical and self-righteous attitudes that some Christians take toward their religious beliefs.

F. Nietzsche was hostile toward Jews.
1. Nietzsche has this reputation because he sometimes refers to the Jews in unflattering terms—as he does everyone else—and because Wagner was an anti-Semite.
2. However, he analyzes Christianity as a sect of Judaism.
3. Nietzsche's critique of Judaism is an aspect of his critique of Christianity.
4. It is also an aspect that would be very galling to anti-Semites.

G. Nietzsche was a Nazi.
1. The Nazi party wasn't formed until 1919, nearly twenty years after Nietzsche's death.
2. His sister Elizabeth married a proto-fascist, and she created his (Nietzsche's) reputation.
3. Nietzsche was largely non-political, and certainly did not admire the German state.

H. Nietzsche was power-mad.
1. His concept of the "will to power" has led many to think he applauded military conquest.
2. Most of the time, Nietzsche uses the term psychologically.

3. Power motivates many human activities beside war and quests for conquest, art for example.

I. Nietzsche favored war, murder, cruelty.
1. Nietzsche served as an orderly, not a soldier. He was not pro-war (but not a pacifist either).
2. He saw cruelty in himself, as in everyone, and was honest (and worried) about that.

J. Nietzsche admired barbarians.
1. Nietzsche admired the ancient Athenians, and one might call them "barbarians."
2. However, he did not encourage brawn without brain.

K. Nietzsche defended eugenics.
1. So did most other intellectuals of his time (e.g., George Bernard Shaw).
2. The term "eugenics" sounds distasteful to us because of the Nazis' experiments.

L. Nietzsche suggests the *Übermensch* as evolutionary goal.
1. Nietzsche was ambivalent about Darwin.
2. He accepted evolution and enjoyed pointing out our animal nature.
3. He did not believe that progress of the (human) species was assured.
4. The *Übermensch* is rarely mentioned in Nietzsche's writing.
5. The *Übermensch* is an ideal for spiritual development— a willingness to take risks for the sake of creating something great, something beyond oneself.

M. Nietzsche was a nihilist.
1. Nihilism (the term comes from Russia) is the rejection of all values.
2. Nietzsche is no nihilist, but rejects nihilistic values.

N. Nietzsche was a relativist.
1. He endorsed relativism in the innocent sense that values are always contextual, relative to a time, a people, a place, and particular circumstances.
2. He rejected relativism in the vulgar sense that insists that every view is as valid (or invalid) as any other.

O. Nietzsche defended selfishness.

1. He rejected the distinction between "selfish" and "selfless."
2. He rather asked, "whose ego?" What is selfish depends on the person.

P. Nietzsche used fallacies in argumentation, such as *ad hominem*.
1. He did indeed, including personal attacks and bald appeal to the emotions of his readers.
2. Nevertheless, these "fallacies" play an important role in his philosophy—and are not fallacies at all.

Q. Nietzsche was a bad historian.
1. In fact, Nietzsche knew history extremely well. He had a good education, an excellent philological background, and training in historical theology.
2. Some contemporary philosophers have dismissed Nietzsche's accounts for their irresponsible representations of history.
3. Some of Nietzsche's accounts are too simplistic if taken to be history. However, Nietzsche tells these tales to bring out particular (polemical) points, particularly in connection with his critique of Christianity.
4. These might be seen as allegories or parables, usually aimed at getting us to see things differently. They are simplistic in order to reverse customary ways of looking at things.

R. Nietzsche wrote only aphorisms.
1. Nietzsche employed a broad range of styles, experimenting throughout his career.
2. His aphoristic style has a very special aim, to force the reader to think for him or herself.

Recommended Reading:

Prefaces to *Daybreak, Gay Science, Beyond Good and Evil.*

Supplemental Reading:

Richard Schacht, *Selections*, Intro., pp. 21–68.

Robert C. Solomon and Kathleen M. Higgins, *What Nietzsche Really Said*, Chapter 1.

Ivan Soll in Richard Schacht, ed., *Nietzsche: Selections*; *Genealogy, Morality*, pp. 168–192.

Questions to Consider:

1. Why does Nietzsche seem open to so many radically different interpretations of his work and his ideas? How does he render himself so prone to abuse?

2. Even if Nietzsche were shown to be crazy during his productive years, would that force us to alter our view of his work?

Lecture Two—Transcript
Quashing the Rumors about Nietzsche

Solomon: Because Nietzsche was so polemical and because he has become so notorious, he has been misunderstood in a good many ways. In fact, there are probably more rumors, myths, and misunderstandings about Nietzsche than about any other philosopher. So what we would like to do in this lecture is to straighten out some of these misunderstandings and talk about the ways in which the rumors of Nietzsche have circulated and why most of them are downright false.

As I suggested in my introduction to the first lecture, I married a Nietzsche scholar, and I would like to introduce her. This is Kathy Higgins, who is my wife and also my colleague. We do spend a lot of time taking about Nietzsche, and what we would like to do is to talk about some of these misunderstandings such as the idea that Nietzsche was crazy, the idea that Nietzsche was a Nazi, the idea that Nietzsche hated women, the idea that Nietzsche hated both Christians and Jews, the idea that he loved barbarians, and so on.

But let's start out with the myth that defines a good deal of the Nietzsche popular culture. It's one that appeared in a philosophy textbook under the following guise: Nietzsche was crazy; therefore, we don't have to take seriously anything he said. I am going to start by asking Kathy, "What about this idea that Nietzsche was crazy?"

Higgins: Well, obviously, if he is crazy as the vernacular for being mentally ill, that does pertain to Nietzsche in the last decade of his life. The big question with regard to the rumor, however, is whether that applies to any of his writings. I think sometimes people have thought that he was crazy because he tends to write in hyperbole and be rather bombastic, sort of praising himself and putting down his opponents, particularly in his autobiography, which he names *Ecce Homo*, actually the words that Pilate spoke to the crowd when presenting Jesus—"Behold the man." He uses a lot of bombast and talks about why he is a destiny, why he writes such good books. "Why I am So Wise" is one of his chapter titles. Actually, I think that what he is pointing to is the fact that anybody writing an autobiography is really trying to tell you what is so wise about them, why they are such a good and interesting person, and Nietzsche is being just a little bit more honest about that, I think, in a joking way.

So, most of the time, what's been sometimes interpreted as his craziness is actually a kind of perverse sense of humor.

At the same time, some people have found that their interest in this is really more lurid than anything because one rumor that I think has a certain amount of basis is the idea that Nietzsche was crazy because he was syphilitic, and that was indeed the diagnosis that was given to him when he was taken to the asylum after his collapse. One question that this immediately sparks is, Well, where did he get syphilis? A possibility is that he inherited it from his father who died when he was young and was diagnosed as having softening of the brain, which is a little hard to quite know how we describe it in the current day. Other rumors, of course, are that Nietzsche contracted this in his adult life. I think the main reason this is a matter of interest to people is really the same kind of sensationalism that drives people to tabloid journalism. What was Nietzsche's sex life like? As a matter of fact, he was pretty discreet on this topic.

Solomon: I think that's right, although there have been speculations recently that Nietzsche's sex life wasn't as empty as we once thought it was. There are rumors today, backed up by some factual considerations, that Nietzsche may have been gay. Given the combination of his discretion and the forbidden nature of such activity in the nineteenth century, that would make a lot of sense. As for his earlier sexual activity, the one story we have is that he was taken to a brothel when he was a fairly young man, and he enjoyed himself by sitting down and playing the piano. I think that summarizes Nietzsche's sex life better than anything else does.

Higgins: Also, I think that, with regard to the rumor that he was gay, he may have been, but it reminds me of a radio show I was listening to one time on a classical station that was having a kind of tribute to Tchaikovsky. Someone phoned in and asked, "Is it true that Tchaikovsky was a homosexual?" The announcer paused and said, "Yes, but that isn't the only reason we admire him." I think that is fairly apt for Nietzsche as well.

Solomon: One of the things, of course, that is most often known about Nietzsche that is still a matter of considerable accusation even by people who should know better is that Nietzsche hated women. He grew up in a family of women, to be sure, but you must take a lot of flak as a female Nietzsche scholar. I am sure people have always asked you questions like, "What is a nice girl like you doing with a clod like him?"

Higgins: Yes, that has kind of plagued my career as a Nietzsche scholar. I think there is a lot to say about it, and I'll say more about it later in the series. One of the things I would like to point out is that Freud was greatly influenced by Nietzsche precisely because Nietzsche was aware of his own problems with women. Nietzsche, for instance, comments, "If you want to know why a man views women the way he does, take a look at his relationship to his mother." I think that's one of the themes, one of many, that Freud picked up on in developing his own theory. So Nietzsche was very self-aware about the fact that his attitudes toward women were complicated and not entirely desirable.

He also does some very interesting things in writing about women, for example, suggesting that one take the motivations of a woman from her own point of view seriously, something I think was kind of unheard of among writers of his period. The main reason—besides some outlandish statements that we will discuss later on—that he has this reputation, I think, is that he was very much opposed to some of the practices and goals of the feminist movement of his day, particularly the desire to make women more like men. From his point of view, his contemporaries in Europe, his male contemporaries, were hardly any role model, and the idea of women also trying to be like men whom he found too conformist to begin with was certainly not going to improve much of anything. So some of this has to do with his general goals for human individuality and diversity. A unisex ideal is far from what he wanted.

Solomon: What about his attitude towards Christianity? Certainly it was hostile; he publishes a good deal that is straightforwardly antagonistic.

Higgins: That is certainly true. Nevertheless, it's important to notice what he is and isn't antagonistic about. As you mentioned, he wasn't particularly antagonistic about the historical Jesus or his insights, but he thought that the development of the church and some of the motivations of church leaders was far from as benign as it posed itself as being. He tends to criticize what Kierkegaard called Christendom—the sort of social practices that have gone on surrounding the Christian religion, institutionalized behavior that really isn't very meaningful to peoples' lives for any but social and even political reasons. A lot of times he thought that what passed itself off as a kind of good way of being, a virtuous way of being, was actually both self-righteous and deeply self-interested. I think one of his great one-liners here is the Christian law of love: "In the end it wants to be paid well." I think maybe that kind of sums up his attitude.

Solomon: His attitude towards the Jews. It's often said that he is anti-Semitic; I have already suggested he is not, but . . .

Higgins: Right. I think one of the reasons—besides his association with Wagner, who was anti-Semitic—for this rumor is that he does talk about the Jews as such at times, and not all of his characterizations are complimentary. On the other hand, almost none of his characterizations of any human group are complimentary. He talks about Germans, Christians, Hindus, and Buddhists. He has caricatures to make of all of these groups and what they pride themselves on. But I think a lot of his comments about the Jews have the very interesting function of really attacking anti-Semites.

Since anti-Semites in his era were very much concerned to separate Christianity from Judaism, usually suggesting that Christianity was the superior way of looking at things, what he keeps drawing attention back to is the fact that Jesus was a Jew, that Christianity began as a Jewish sect. So frequently, when he says something about the Jewish way of looking at the world, he makes it very clear that he isn't separating Christianity from this Jewish tradition and is reminding anti-Semites over and over again, "Well, of course one would expect Jesus to say this, being a Jew." It sounds like an anti-Semitic line, but, actually, I think it's an attack on those who pride themselves as being followers of Jesus, not anything Jewish.

Solomon: Then, of course, there's the rumor that Nietzsche was a Nazi. Just to say the obvious—to begin with, the Nazi party didn't come into existence until 1919, and, of course, Hitler didn't come to power until 1933. Nietzsche was dead by 1900 and was out of his mind by 1889. He was very unsympathetic, in fact, to what we might call the proto-Nazi movement. He broke with his sister over precisely this issue. He hated his brother-in-law for the same reason. And it's Elizabeth who, edited some of Nietzsche's works, particularly the non-book, *The Will to Power*, which is published as a Nietzsche book but, in fact, was just a bunch of his notes that is often used to convey the impression that he supported some of her fascist politics. He did not. In fact, I think Nietzsche was virtually apolitical. With some stretching, you can find some political comments. He certainly is anti-Bismarck and antimilitarism and anti-German nationalism. But if he had a politics at all, I think the thing to say is that it would be the politics of ancient Greece, a kind of aristocracy, which literally means "rule by the best." But that's the very antithesis, of course, of what the Nazis had.

Higgins: Of course, Nietzsche's slogan, "will to power," does tend to reinforce the image of Nietzsche as, if not proto-Nazi, at least favoring the kinds of abuses that the Nazis were guilty of. It sounds, for instance, like a defense of power politics. And Nietzsche's attitude, I think, toward politics is that it is an expression of will to power. Will to power, as he sees it, is a kind of description of a generic motivation for human beings and basically all biological beings to enhance their life. Certainly, if you are talking about political battle and entrenchment, the idea of sort of being on the offense rather than the defense strikes a lot of politicians as reasonable and would strike Nietzsche as a manifestation of this drive to enhance your situation.

But when he talks about will to power, it often is not politics he has in mind at all, or anything related to military conquest as it's sometimes been thought. In fact, probably his most frequent type of example would be the will to power manifest by artists who want to extend their influence broader than it would be if they were just people without any kind of further way of communicating with the world. So power he sees on all kinds of levels—certainly not something that he sees as especially a matter of politics—and often politicians strike him as inordinately crude and unsubtle in their efforts and therefore as not very effective.

Solomon: Nietzsche also, of course, has a reputation as a warmonger. It's not hard to understand where that comes from. During the First World War, the Kaiser's troops were carrying around copies of his book, *Thus Spoke Zarathustra,* in their knapsacks. Nevertheless, Nietzsche himself was certainly not pro-war. He served as an orderly in the Franco-Prussian War, not as a soldier. If anything, Nietzsche despised war, and he despised the kinds of motives that gave rise to it, the nationalism, the chauvinism, and so on. Nevertheless, Nietzsche had a very competitive notion of life, the idea of life as a struggle, and he also suggested that we take a much more realistic view of human life and human nature than most moralists were prone to do.

In particular, he has several passages where he talks at great length about cruelty, something that most moralists mention only by way of saying how horrible it is. Well, without denying its horror, Nietzsche also wants to point out what a major role it has played in human life, and he himself, in himself, saw that it is much more complicated than moralists would make it out to be. He says, for example, in a letter of 1882, "One gets to love something, and one hardly has begun to love it profoundly when the tyrant in us, which we call our higher self, says, 'Sacrifice that to me.' I tell you frankly that I have in myself much of this tragic complexion. To be able not to curse it, I would like to take away from human existence some of its heartbreaking and cruel character."

Nietzsche didn't admire barbarians. What he admired was dynamic life. And dynamic life, unfortunately, includes some cruelty. But the people he admires—we are not talking about Conan—we are talking about people like Goethe, the great German poet, or perhaps Beethoven, artists who excel, who fight not with other people, who fight not between themselves but, rather, who fight with the envelope of creativity. That's what he is really talking about.

Higgins: I think he also appreciated the way that war sometimes brings out in people's character a real commitment, a willingness to really throw your life and even risk your life for something. That's something that we will see repeatedly as major value in a positive sense for Nietzsche. But, as far as defending him against the charge that he admires barbarians, what about the opposite charge that he really wants to bring about a super race?

Solomon: Well, Nietzsche is often condemned as a eugenicist, someone who believed in breeding the right kind of person. I think this is a view that is colored by the fact that we are looking back through the Nazis and the awful things they did in the names of eugenics and euthanasia and the master race. But, of course, if we are thinking around the period of 1880 or so, Nietzsche was just one of many, many European intellectuals who thought that breeding a better kind of person and discouraging the proliferation of weaker, more troublesome, asocial types of human beings was a good idea. For example, the socialist George Bernard Shaw in England was an avid eugenicist, and no one would say of him that he was a proto-

Nazi. So I think one has to be very careful about how this is interpreted. Nevertheless, he does have this famous concept of the Übermensch, the super man, and he often does seem to be presenting that as a desirable replacement for humanity.

Higgins: I don't know if I would go along with the way of breeding which, admittedly, he sets up, which is to say that this is a kind of replacement or an evolutionary goal. I think he is very happy when he presents the notion of the super man or Übermensch as a kind of future that's beyond the human future, and that it does sound evolutionary—and he certainly does think we want to consciously intervene to make the species better—but, nevertheless, I think he is trying to do a couple of things with this image. One is to suggest that his nineteenth-century contemporaries who view the human race as the product of the fruit of nature, the ultimate, are wrong.

He, like most of his contemporaries in intellectual fields, does believe at least that much of Darwin, that the human race evolved from lower species, but he doesn't want to suggest that this is the triumph of nature. If anything, he is interested in pointing out that people are often human, all too human, and we ought to try to move beyond our present state of existence. He is happy to point out that there is a kind of continuity between us and animals. So, in that sense, too, I think he kind of likes the ring of the evolutionary in this image.

But, if anything, I think the rare context in which this image even comes up is almost exclusively in a very early part of *Thus Spoke Zarathustra*—the primary discussion is in the prologue. In those contexts, it's very clear that he has this in mind as a kind of goal for spiritual accomplishment, the idea of trying to stake your life on creating a better world and creating a possibility of greatness that nobody has achieved so far. He is very worried that we aren't going to have a kind of evolutionary outcome where something superior is going to develop but instead that it's going to be a matter of devolution.

Solomon: This image also belies the rumor that Nietzsche is a kind of a nihilist. As I said in the first lecture, I think nothing is further from the truth, and the notion of the Übermensch, not just what Nietzsche particularly says about it but his whole notion of striving higher and being more than we currently are, suggests that Nietzsche is profoundly committed to a set of values, whereas nihilism is the opposite thesis. There are no values. There is nothing worth committing ourselves to. In contemporary life, I think the attitude that tragically displays this quite pervasively is cynicism. It's a way of saying nothing really matters; the future really is irrelevant and may not be there at all. Nietzsche is absolutely against this whole notion. He is not ready to say there are no values. To the contrary, what he wants to say is the values that we do accept, the sorts of values that lead to cynicism, those are the ones to be attacked in favor of real values, values that are worth defending, and, ultimately, the value of life itself.

Higgins: Well, you might think that that's a kind of universal value, but clearly he makes it obvious that he thinks people not only have sometimes had different kinds of values but that this might be a good thing. So what about the charge that he is really a rampant relativist?

Solomon: Well, relativism is a much more interesting version of nihilism because it doesn't say there are no values. It says there are lots of values, and, in fact, Nietzsche is a pluralist as Wayne James was about the same time. The idea is that there is no one right morality; there is no one right to live. Rather, the way to live is according to one's context, one's culture, one's time, and so on. Now, relativism is often misunderstood by philosophers and by other people as well. There is, of course, a very strong movement in the United States right now in favor of absolute values, although, when pressed to spell out what that means, often its defenders retreat to some rather banal clichés about religion and so on.

The truth is that relativism is, in one sense, an irrefutable, simply self-evident thesis. And that is that values are relative to the people, the times, and the conditions; that values are not simply writ large for everyone. Insofar as we have such overriding values like do no harm, don't kill people without a good reason, and don't take other people's property, the truth is that these are interpreted and reinterpreted in many, many different ways according to different cultures. But there is a vicious notion of relativism that borders on nihilism, and that's the idea that relativism is any view—any perspective is as good as any other one.

Well, I find this a deplorable thesis, but Nietzsche did, too. If there is one thing that you realize as you read through Nietzsche's works, even if he often presents different sides of an issue, it's very clear that he thinks that some positions are better than others, that some forms of morality are far superior to others. So, in terms of relativism, I would say, well, yes, he is a relativist in the benign, obvious sense. He is very sensitive to differences between people and peoples, but in the vicious sense, the sense in which relativism blends into nihilism, no, he is not at all.

Higgins: I think actually a lot of people who have read Nietzsche to a certain extent would criticize the values that he does think are better than others, particularly his high evaluation of promoting yourself. Is he really a defender of selfishness?

Solomon: Well, he certainly made out that way. The contemporary philosopher Ayn Rand, who is very popular in some American circles, well, she doesn't approve of Nietzsche because I think she realizes that he said what she was trying to say much better. Nevertheless, there is an affinity between the two of them, which I think she vulgarizes. She says that selfishness is a kind of virtue and it's to be contrasted with a sense of self-sacrifice. Nietzsche, I think, is much more subtle and much more sophisticated. What Nietzsche wants to say in a way is that the notion of selfishness itself is something that we should examine, that we should examine the supposed opposition between selfishness on the one hand and altruism or self-sacrifice on the other.

The truth is that, with a noble temperament, what you do that might seem like a self-sacrifice to others is, in fact, what you perceive as being in your own best interest because this is an expression of the kind of person you are. The question for selfishness, with Nietzsche—which he puts in a very simple, pithy question—the question isn't just egoism, the question is always "whose ego?" If what we are talking about is the self-absorption and the sort of almost fanatic self-pursuit of, say, a great artist, say Mozart trying to write the perfect piece of music or Goethe or Hertel trying to write the perfect poem, well, there is nothing selfish about that even though, in an obvious sense, it's doing what they most want to do, everyone else be damned. But at the same time, there is a kind petty selfishness. It's the selfishness of slave morality, it's the selfishness of "you can't have that because I want it, and I am jealous or envious of you." That's the kind of selfishness that Nietzsche rejects.

Higgins: Well, one of the things that Nietzsche is criticized for as well are many of the features of the way he writes and not just the kind of mad quality. I think a related point connected to the selfishness idea and the question of whose ego is that he makes a lot of references in his writings to the type of person that would hold a particular philosophy, often one he doesn't think much of. What do you think about this whole strategy? After all, isn't it a fallacy to claim that you shouldn't believe anything Nietzsche writes because, after all, he was insane?

Solomon: Well, it certainly is a fallacy, but I have a question about a lot of the fallacies that philosophers and rhetoricians talk about, and that is, Are they really fallacies? Are they always fallacies? With reference to at ad hominem arguments, which is what you are talking about in particular, the idea of attacking the person instead of talking about the argument or talking about the position, well, there's a sense in which that cuts through all of Nietzsche's philosophy. When he says, for example, that the philosopher is to be evaluated along with the philosophy, that you can judge the philosopher by the philosophy and the philosophy by the philosopher, that means it doesn't make sense to just look at an abstract philosophical thesis. You want to know, "Who wrote it? Why did he or she write it? When did he or she write it? What were the conditions, the circumstances, the influences? What's the thesis trying to prove in a personal way?"

As I said, in *Beyond Good and Evil*, one of the theses that Nietzsche throws out first is that philosophy is ultimately a confession; philosophy is ultimately a kind of memoir, even if it's not intended that way. So, from that point of view, you want to say an ad hominem argument can be very revealing. For example, he says that Socrates is ugly. Now that's something that is intended to drive philosophers, and especially philosophers who love the ancients, up a tree, but, of course, he wants to make an important point out of this. The fact that Socrates was ugly, the fact that he was, as Nietzsche says, lower class, really explains an awful lot of his most profound ideas. Or he says of Kant a good deal about what does it take for a person to want to believe in that kind of absolute universal morality. The answer is naturally going to be ad hominem. Or my favorite— talking about German philosophy in general, he says there is too much beer in the German intellect. That explains an awful lot when you think about it.

But it is not just ad hominem arguments, of course. Another fallacy that every undergraduate is warned against is you don't appeal to emotions—to which Nietzsche and I would want to ask, What do you appeal to? Pure logic, pure rationality? Appeal to the emotions is precisely what it takes to move someone to get them to think about their lives and to get them to change it. So I would say, as for the fallacies, this is part of Nietzsche's style, part of his rhetorical strategy, but I don't want to be too quick to condemn it. I think it's something one should be cautious about, but it serves a very important purpose.

Higgins: Well, at least the idea that Socrates was ugly is documented in a number of ancient texts, but some people have criticized Nietzsche also for coming up with historical models that aren't very detailed. I mean, after all, *Birth and Tragedy* didn't include the footnotes that many of his colleagues hoped it would, and he does tend to play a little fast and loose with historical facts. I think a way to read Nietzsche on history, especially when he makes grand pronouncements about certain areas producing slave morality, the morality of the underdog as opposed to those in power having their own master morality—Many historians would quarrel with the exact date at which any such event might have occurred and suggest that this is a vast oversimplification. Fair enough, but Nietzsche isn't really trying to present a kind of documented story where every detail is taken into account—is that he is trying to create images that will cause people to rethink history. I mean, after all, he is referring oftentimes to pretty well-known parts of the European background.

So, for instance, when he says Socrates is ugly, this is something that's on record, and he draws attention to this fact and says, well, maybe this ought to change the way we look at that whole experience. I mean, what was a man like this doing, leading the Athenians? Why was he the hero of the youth? I mean, after all, young people at the time tended to view older men as having a kind of wisdom but even more wisdom if they were good-looking. Maybe we still think that today. So how did this happen? In other words, what Nietzsche is trying to do here is draw attention to a period where people already have some insights and, through these kinds of quick, fast stories about motivation, suggest that we really rethink it. They have the function more of parables, I think, trying to draw something new into the foreground for us; they are not anything like a kind of detailed historical tract.

Solomon: Nietzsche's style is certainly unusual. It's the most striking thing when one picks up a book by him. One sees, first of all, aphorisms. One sees lots of exclamation points, something that's unusual in philosophy. One sees lots of italics, French and Latin phrases all over the place. But the idea that Nietzsche's style somehow renders him less philosophical, a charge we often hear, or makes him merely a poet or a literary writer rather than a philosopher, that's something we certainly want to reject because what the style does is it reflects ideas.

In particular, Nietzsche is famous for his aphoristic style, but the mistake is to think that this is all he does. Even in the aphoristic books, which are really the middle period, the period of *Human, All Too Human*, *Daybreak*, and *Gay Science*, even there there's a strategy. There is a detailed organization, and, of course, there's an overwhelming purpose, and it's a philosophical purpose. It's to jar us into thinking in a certain way. But other books consist of essays, and some books consist of long meditations, so it's a mistake to think of Nietzsche's style as just one thing.

Lecture Three
The Fusion of Philosophy and Psychology

Scope:

Nietzsche prided himself on his fusion of philosophy and psychology. At one point, he even absurdly brags, "I am the first philosopher to also be a psychologist." He attempts not to justify human beliefs and practices but, like a psychoanalytically trained anthropologist, to *explain* them in terms of personality and character. He is not alone in this method. His near contemporary, the Danish philosopher Søren Kierkegaard, was also a brilliant philosopher-psychologist. So was his English nemesis, John Stuart Mill, and his German mentor, Schopenhauer. But Nietzsche anticipated Freud and psychoanalysis in a way that was, as Freud admitted, uncanny.

Outline

I. Nietzsche synthesized philosophy and psychology and used psychological analyses to explain (rather than justify) philosophical doctrines and arguments.

  A. Nietzsche pioneered the psychoanalysis of morals, arguing that morality must be understood in terms of the aspirations and fears of the people who embrace it rather than its supposedly divine or rational origins.

  B. He insisted on naturalistic explanations of morality and religious belief and he was not concerned to justify morality, as Kant was.

  C. Nietzsche believed that compassion, pity, and benevolence constitute an assertion of power over others.

II. Nietzsche rejected the English Utilitarian view of ethics.

  A. The English Utilitarians assumed that happiness or pleasure (and the avoidance of pain) was the ultimate motive of all human behavior. Nietzsche suggests that it is "the will to power."

  B. In his treatment of pity (compassion, *Mitleid*), Nietzsche shows us how a seemingly innocent and noble moral attitude can in fact be seen as disturbing and base.

III. Nietzsche diagnosed some of the prevalent moral theorists as well.

    A. He came to view Schopenhauer's pessimism as a psychological problem.

    B. He diagnosed Socrates as a man who ultimately hated life and sought respite in the "otherworldly."

    C. He most famously diagnosed Christian morality as a "slave morality," and Christians as weak human beings.

        1. Nietzsche held that people accepted Christian morality because of their fear of being shunned by others.

        2. The Christian virtues are virtues of weakness.

IV. Nietzsche echoes and anticipates some of the most profound psychologists of modern times.

    A. Nietzsche has deep insights into the relation between religion and *angst*.

        1. Nietzsche can be compared with his Danish colleague Søren Kierkegaard. Unlike Nietzsche, however, Kierkegaard was devoutly religious; nonetheless, the thinkers shared many beliefs.

        2. For example, they had similar views about Christendom and Christianity as a "herd religion" animated by peer pressure more than by spiritual concerns.

        3. Nietzsche can also be compared with his Russian contemporary, Fyodor Dostoevsky.

        4. Both Kierkegaard and Dostoevsky analyzed dread or "*angst*," and they were aware of its importance in human life.

    B. He also bears comparison to Feuerbach, Marx, and Freud in his development of his attitude of "deep suspicion."

        1. Like Feuerbach (who influenced Marx), Nietzsche interpreted the world materialistically, in terms of this world, rather than another.

        2. Like Marx, Nietzsche insisted that what people believe depends upon their conditions of life.

        3. Like Freud, Nietzsche insisted that most of what motivates our behavior is unconscious; both were skeptical of people's stated motivations.

Essential Reading:

Beyond Good and Evil, Sect. I.

R. J. Hollingdale, ed., *A Nietzsche Reader*, "Philosophy and Philosophers,"
pp. 29–52, and "Psychological Observations," pp. 149–166.

Daybreak and *Human, All Too Human* in Schacht, ed., *Nietzsche: Selections* (*Daybreak*, Book II).

Supplemental Reading:

Frithjof Bergmann, in Robert C. Solomon, Kathleen M. Higgins, *Reading Nietzsche*, pp. 29–45.

Richard Schacht, ed., *Genealogy, Morality*; *Nietzsche: Selections*, pp. 237–247 and 139–167.

Questions to Consider:

1. Are compassion and pity always or even usually noble or commendable emotions? In what ways can they go wrong?

2. Do you think that people basically live for pleasure (and the avoidance of pain)? Does it make sense to say that what they live for is *power*?

Lecture Three—Transcript
The Fusion of Philosophy and Psychology

One of the keys to understanding Nietzsche is to understand that he is both a philosopher and a psychologist. In fact, he says at one point he is the first philosopher to be a great psychologist. This I think is absurd. One can trace the connection between philosophy and psychology all the way back to the Greeks. Certainly the medieval Christians were philosophers who were almost obsessed with human psychology, and, in the modern period, we have people like John Locke, and, just before Nietzsche, of course, there's Schopenhauer. Nevertheless, I think the connection is an important one, and it's particularly striking if we think in historical terms because, until the twentieth century, really, the distinction between philosophy and psychology was not at all defined. I often joke that it is really academic administrations and probably worrying faculty members that pushed the two subjects apart from one another.

I think the truth is that every great philosopher always has also been a psychologist, but I think Nietzsche does deserve some credit as being perhaps the most insightful and the most profound of all of them. He synthesized philosophy and psychology in a number of different ways. One might say that what he gave us was a psychoanalysis of morals, a psychoanalysis of religion, and, in this, he anticipates most obviously Freud and some of the psychoanalysts who came after Freud. But I think a very clear way of putting this without falling into any kind of psychoanalytic jargon is to say that the way Nietzsche thought of his own thinking is that it had to be strictly naturalistic.

Now what that means on the one hand is that it's natural as opposed to supernatural, that explanations had to be in human terms, or at least biological, earthly terms rather than theological terms. If you want to talk about morality, then don't talk about its divine origins but, rather, talk about the human motivations that underlie it. Or, to put it in a different way, what Nietzsche wants to do is to explain morality. Most philosophers, by contrast, have tried to justify it. Immanuel Kant for example, one of the very great philosophers of the modern period and probably pretty arguably the greatest German philosopher before Nietzsche, had a thesis that essentially said that morality is a matter of reason and reason, of course, is something that was put in us by God. But, also, Kant tried to justify morality. In fact, a good third of his great philosophy is devoted to just that: to understand exactly why morality is necessary for rational beings.

What Nietzsche wants to do, by contrast, is to explain why not such rational beings as ourselves would be moved to accept morality or, to put it more precisely in ways that we'll explain later, why they would be inclined to accept a set of rules that were quite distinctively to their own immediate, individual disadvantage. So what we are going to be looking for, for Nietzsche, is a way of understanding morality, a way of understanding religious belief in psychological terms. A few examples: One can think, for example, of the idea that we are naturally inclined to be kind, that we are naturally inclined to be compassionate, something that a great many philosophers have argued and hoped for. The ancient philosophers—Mencius in China—argued such a thesis. The economist Adam Smith, who was also a great moral philosopher, argued such a thesis, and, more immediately, Schopenhauer, Nietzsche's mentor, had argued such a thesis.

What Nietzsche points out is, if you really examine pity, compassion, sympathy, and the like, what you find is something very different. What you find, among other things, is a search for individual superiority, an assertion of individual power, if it is, nevertheless, a kind of impotent and pretty pathetic power. But when you are compassionate towards someone, when you have pity for someone, there is a sense in which what you're doing is making yourself a superior. Or, if you're kind to someone, if you exercise the virtue called benevolence, the truth is what you're doing is asserting and reinforcing a certain amount of power you have over that person—if nothing else, the power to be able to give him something. But, of course, the same is true in the negative side. If you're cruel to someone, what follows is that you are asserting your power, again in a petty, perhaps reprehensible, way. Cruelty and benevolence both are, in effect, exercises of power, and the idea of personal power, asserting one's strength, is something that pervades Nietzsche's psychology. In fact, it is its primary principle.

This gives rise to an obvious contrast. One of the philosophies that was most prevalent in Nietzsche's time—in fact, it is still prevalent today—was the mainly English philosophy called utilitarianism, the idea that what people are motivated by is pleasure or the avoidance of pain. What people really want is happiness, and the way to understand their behavior is by that, to understand how certain courses of action, perhaps long-term courses of action, make for more pleasure, for less pain, for more happiness. Nietzsche says, rather strikingly, that actually this is a very poor explanation of most human behavior. Human beings often do what will make them unhappy. For example, they act out of spite, they act out of resentment, they act out of envy, and these things don't make anyone happier, but what they all do in one way or another, sometimes very deviously, is they assert a person's power.

Nietzsche's attitude towards utilitarianism is, like most German philosophers of the time, largely dismissive. He finds it vulgar. One of Nietzsche's best lines, in my view, is when he says, "Man does not seek happiness; only the Englishman does." It is a kind of direct attack on Nietzsche's nemesis—although one sometimes wonders why—John Stuart Mill, who was probably the greatest English philosopher of the late nineteenth century and, in a way, Nietzsche's direct competitor. But the competition really was between two different theories, a theory of power and a theory of pleasure. The one theory said that people are basically motivated by hedonism, the desire for happiness. The other said that a good deal of human behavior, if not all of human behavior, and, by the way, animal behavior, too, can much better be explained as the pursuit of some sort of power, self-expression, or assertion.

Nietzsche considers, for example, people who defended what we would today call animal rights. Nietzsche himself was certainly not cruel and, in particular, had a certain kind of affection for animals, as I mentioned in the first lecture. When he collapsed on the street of Italy, he was hugging a horse to prevent it from a beating. Nevertheless, looking very skeptically at animal rights advocates, what he suggests, and I am sure we can all think of examples, is that people who are so gung ho about animal rights are really betraying a kind of hatred of their fellow human beings, that what they are doing is displacing. What looks like love, in fact, is something very much like hatred. He also says that, of morality in general, we think of people being moral because they are obeying the rules or because they are being reasonable, or simply because they are going along with what everyone else thinks they ought to do.

But what Nietzsche points out is that what really drives us to behave morally is our enormous fear of solitude, of being shunned, of being left alone. Once again, if you examine your own motives in doing the right thing, in at least some occasions, what you realize is that the dominant motivation—we are not talking about justification—the dominant motivation, the dominant explanation is the fact that we are afraid we will lose our friends, that people won't talk to us. In Tom Wolfe's new book, *A Man in Full*, the lead character at the very end has to make what amounts to the decision of his life, and the primary motive that clearly drives him is he is afraid of taking that one stand because he'll lose his friends, the people who now talk to him. The people who now go hunting and fishing and are his buddies will no longer respect him.

Nietzsche wants to say solitude is a very important aspect of human life. Solitude, more importantly, is a very important element in integrity, in the extent to which we are willing to lose our friends. To be shunned is just that kind of motivation we need to be able to tell the truth. Nietzsche's philosophy, which often turns out to be harsh and polemical, to say things that other people won't say, has to be understood in part in terms of the rejection of that sense that being shunned, being ignored, is the worst thing that can happen to us. That's not to say that Nietzsche didn't want to be read, and that he didn't resent, as his career unfolded, the fact that his books were not being bought. Nevertheless, to understand Nietzsche is to understand just how important that emphasis on peer pressure, that emphasis on social solidarity, must have been first to him, but, secondly, how much he saw that that is the dominant motive of so much of our behavior.

Nietzsche uses this psychological/philosophical kind of mix to understand morality in general and to understand the work of particular philosophers. For example, trying to understand Schopenhauer and Schopenhauer's pessimism in particular, one can easily understand why Nietzsche would be almost obsessed with the question, Why would a person defend a philosophy that basically says life is no good? What must it be about the philosopher that promotes that view? Trying to understand that, very clearly, is a form of psychoanalysis.

Perhaps it comes through most clearly in Nietzsche's most frequent target—also, in a sense, his most frequent hero—and that's in his diagnosis of Socrates. We already mentioned that Nietzsche says, rather outrageously, that Socrates was ugly, but that, of course, is one piece of a larger picture. Socrates hates life. Now, that's not the way we usually think of Socrates. In Plato's dialogues, Socrates is usually buoyant, almost buffoonish. He is man-about-town, he is the gadfly, he is the person who wants to talk to everyone and seems to be enjoying his life immensely, and yet Nietzsche looks very skeptically and critically at the philosophy, which says, among other things, that the way we should view ourselves is not in terms of this earthly social body, but, rather, the way we should view ourselves is in terms of this eternal soul, something that clearly is going to carve the way for Christianity.

What's more, we should think of the real world not in terms of this changing world that we live in, in which things are born and grow and decay and die, but, rather, we should think of the real world as a perfect world, a world in which only perfect ideals exist, of which this world is really only a shadow. And Nietzsche asks the question, What would make a philosopher think in such terms? And here the diagnosis comes home. Socrates hated life. However happy, joyful, sociable he may have seemed, the truth is Socrates was looking for another world. And you can anticipate what his primary objective in attacking Christianity is going to be, that, basically, Christianity rejects this world with all of its sufferings, with death, and replaces it with a fantasy, a fantasy that there is no death, a fantasy of a world in which there is no change, in which people don't suffer, in which all of this that we're going through now will somehow be eclipsed and perhaps forgotten.

That is a rationalization, and, again, it is a kind of explanation. Nietzsche does not try to justify morality. He just wants to explain it. There is another sense in which Nietzsche diagnoses Christianity, and Christian morality in particular, as a kind of a slave morality. I have mentioned this, and I am going to be talking about it in great detail later on, but—just to anticipate—in the same way, what Nietzsche wants to do is ask the question, Why would people accept what they call morality? And, of course, one piece of it is what I already said, and that is that people are afraid of being shunned; they're afraid of being pushed aside and ignored, of being left alone. In that sense, Nietzsche points out that what we call morality is really a herd morality. What we really want is to remain like everyone else or at least to be liked by everyone else.

There is a deeper sense, though, in which, if you think of the particular values of Christianity, such notions as humility and meekness—what David Hume, an earlier philosopher, had referred to as the monkish virtues—what one starts to suspect is that, although these present themselves as virtues of strength, the truth is they're virtues of weakness. So the diagnosis here is that Christian morality in general should be understood in psychological terms, and those psychological terms are largely going to be diagnostic in terms of human foibles, in terms of human weakness, in terms of what Nietzsche generally calls the "human all too human."

Now let me say that this isn't entirely dismissive because the other side of this is to appreciate what is done out of strength—what Nietzsche refers to in many of his works as the noble way of living—and he wants to understand that psychology, too. There is a sense in which he very clearly anticipates modern psychology, not just Freud, whom I will come back to in a moment, but also some other figures who are very important and, in fact, anticipate Nietzsche in some important ways. The first to be mentioned here is a Danish philosopher who will come up again. Kathy mentioned him in the last lecture. His name is Soren Kierkegaard. He was a philosopher in the middle of the nineteenth century, so just before Nietzsche by a few decades. It is pretty clear that Nietzsche did not have a chance to read him, although he may have heard of him.

Kierkegaard, unlike Nietzsche, was a devoutly religious philosopher, but, in some very interesting ways, they agreed, and, in fact, they're both often classified as existentialists, something which I'll question later on. But the basic idea, which was really created by another German psychologist in the twentieth century named Karl Jaspers, was that, for all of their obvious disagreements—Kierkegaard being a devout Christian, Nietzsche being a rather rampant atheist—for all their apparent disagreements, they really were much more in agreement than not, for example, in their attitude towards what they both, but Kierkegaard in particular, called Christendom or, less flatteringly still, the Christian mob, the idea of Christianity as a herd religion.

Kathy mentioned in the last lecture the fact that what Nietzsche really despised about Christianity was much more the kind of social institutions, and, in particular, what he wanted to say was that Christianity as we know it—and Kierkegaard said much the same thing—Christianity as we know it is really more of a social institution, almost like a club, a somewhat exclusive club and it's meant more for the mutual self-righteousness and aggrandizement of its members than it is, as it states, for a kind of appreciation of something divine, spiritual, and so on.

Kierkegaard, too, is a profound depth psychologist. He analyzes the motives behind most people and their kind of hypocritical Christianity in terms of human weaknesses like laxity and laziness, and, of course, hypocrisy itself can be a powerful motive. Nietzsche follows him, and I think, in many ways, they agree that what Christianity does and the way Christianity must be understood is largely in terms of social peer pressure and not in terms of any particular kind of theological or even psychological motive for spirituality. Kierkegaard, of course, attacks this by way of recreating a genuine notion of Christianity. Nietzsche attacks it in order to put down Christianity for certain purposes, but, nevertheless, I think the two should be seen as akin, and I think the two should be seen as two of the great psychologists behind morality in religion in the modern period.

The other figure that comes to mind here is the Russian novelist Fyodor Dostoevsky. Dostoevsky with Kierkegaard, both had a profound insight into the nature of despair or the emotion that these days is generally referred to in the German style as "angst," anguish, anxiety. Kierkegaard, for example, wrote an entire book, his first book, on the concept of dread. Dostoevsky, in such novels as *The Brothers Karamazov*, in particular, characterizes the same kind of depth psychology and talks about the intense fear, the anxiety of the possibility of facing life without God. Brother Ivan Karamazov essentially says in a famous line, which is often attributed to Nietzsche, "If there is no God, everything is permitted," but, in Ivan's mouth, this is certainly not a kind of joyous cheerfulness as it will be for Nietzsche in a sense, but, rather, it is a cry of despair. Not surprisingly, Ivan goes crazy by the end of the novel.

Both Dostoevsky and Kierkegaard were keenly aware of the role of fear and anxiety in human life, and Nietzsche reinforces this. He talks about the fear of solitude; he talks about the fear of human nature itself, of the passions, of the forces within us that we don't really understand, and, here, of course, he anticipates two of the greatest thinkers in this tradition: one a contemporary, namely, Karl Marx, and the other immediately following him, Sigmund Freud. I'll talk about Marx first because it is a much simpler conversation. It might seem a little bit mysterious that Marx and Nietzsche are put together in the same breath. In fact, Nietzsche hated socialism, he despised democracy, and Marx, in an obvious way, was sensitive and in favor of them both.

But they agreed in something else that was more fundamental, and, in this, they could trace their origins to an earlier German philosopher at the beginning of the nineteenth century, a man named Ludwig Feuerbach. He followed such idealists as Hegel and Kant, who argued that the world consisted mainly of ideas, that what was primarily real was the human mind. What Feuerbach replaced it with was a conception that what the world is, basically, is matter, and what human beings are, basically, is matter in motion. If you want to understand human beings, don't ask first, What do they believe? If you want to understand a human being, ask first, What does he eat? Feuerbach defends a notorious pun in German "Man is was man isst", and what that means basically is one is what one eats.

It's a defense of a basic kind of materialism, not crude materialism in the sense that we sometimes use that term today, namely, somebody who worries only about material goods, cars, sofas, stereos, and the like, but, rather, it's materialism in a basic philosophical sense that the world is straightforwardly matter. The world can be understood in terms of physics and biology. It is perfectly of a piece with Nietzsche's emphasis on naturalism, which, in this interpretation, means, very straightforwardly, if you want to understand human behavior, if you want to understand human motivation, then look to biology, look to physics, look to the kind of energies, look to the kind of motivations, the instincts that biology gives us, and that's where you will understand why people are the way they are.

Feuerbach came crashing into Germany and caused immediate scandals. He had some very important followers, one of whom, of course, was Karl Marx. Marx was also a materialist. He talked about himself as standing Hegel on his head, and what he meant by that was Hegel had talked about the world in terms of ideas; what came first and foremost were the material circumstances of a person's life. And so Marx then essentially becomes an economist. He was early on a Romantic philosopher, but, in his mature years, and as we know him, Marx becomes an economist, and what he starts talking about are the material conditions of life, the forces of production, how economics sort of sets the basis upon which everything else—religion, philosophy, culture, art—is based.

Which brings us to Freud. Freud was also a materialist in this sense. One of his first writings, a work that he never actually published but was certainly published fairly soon after, was a scientific project for making a materialist psychology. The very word *psychology* comes from the study of the psyche, the study of the mind. Freud, of course, kept that, but one of his first projects was a kind of equation between the mind and the brain. Now, without going into much detail here, one can say that, at the end of the nineteenth century, one of the things that was happening was the discovery of neurology, and with the discovery of neurology in its modern sense came the possibility of understanding not just human behavior in its more obvious physical aspects but human behavior in terms of its most intellectual productions—understanding it all in terms of biology.

This is something that Nietzsche clearly endorsed, and Freud, in fact, admits that he picked up a good many of his ideas from Nietzsche. In fact, he even says he stopped reading Nietzsche at a certain point because he realized that, if he kept reading, he would find nothing original to say. But the idea is that what they shared in common—the reason why Nietzsche is so important for understanding modern psychology—is that he did have, as Marx had, a kind of deep skeptical attitude towards people's stated motivations. Rationalization, intellectualization, just played too profound a role. There are certain ways we would like to think of ourselves; there are certain motives that we would like to think move us, when, in fact, this is just a cover story.

When, for example, what we feel is compassion—and, of course, we would like to think of ourselves as compassionate creatures—if you look more closely, what you often find is that, instead of compassion, it's different modes of selfishness, different modes of exerting your superiority or your power. If you defend a cause, it might be a very moral cause. You might have a perfectly good justification for it, but, if you look for the motivation behind your behavior, what you'll often see is something very different. This is sometimes called, rather pretentiously, the hermeneutics of suspicion. It is something that Marx excelled in. It is something that Freud would excel in, but the main figure here has to be Nietzsche.

What it means is, don't accept people's stated motivation at face value. People are not, as earlier philosophers had sometimes argued, in a privileged position—in fact, even in an unmistakable position—to understand why do they do the things they do. To put it in terms that Freud would use, motivation is often unconscious. It is least accessible to the person who is actually doing the deed, and it sometimes takes enormous effort, certainly on the part of that person himself or herself, to understand what it is that's making them do what they do. From a third-person point of view, of course, you don't get the same kind of resistance.

Nevertheless, if what you are trying to understand is human motivation in general, because we are inevitably talking about ourselves as a member of the species, that same resistance sets in, which is why the philosophers of the eighteenth century in particular were so fond about talking about the natural compassion, the natural sympathy that motivated us all, about the natural fellow feeling, sort of community sensibility that motivated human behavior. But, as Nietzsche is quick to point out, what is called community sensibility might also be called herd mentality, the fear of being alone, the desperate fear of solitude.

In the same way, when people talk about themselves as loving, well it's not that Nietzsche attacks love. Certainly he himself fell in love a couple of times, and there is a sense in which he could be a loving person, more generally and more philosophically. He certainly saw certain kinds of love that were highly virtuous, very noble, but what is often called love—something like pity or compassion—is, deep down, petty, selfish, a kind of possessiveness. He says, for example, if you think about romantic love, sexual love, what could be more possessive than that? And we talk about being completely selfless—the truth is there is nothing more selfish than love. So, anticipating Freud, Nietzsche wants to say philosophers must be psychologists. They must try to explain human behavior, including one's own human behavior, and one has to try to not give a whitewash rationalization but instead try to understand what is really going on. That question, "What's really going on?" is precisely what we are going to be talking about for the next several lectures.

Thank you.

Lecture Four
"God Is Dead"—Nietzsche and Christianity

Scope:

Nietzsche famously announced that "God is Dead." This is by no means merely a thesis about religion and religious belief. It relates to the whole mind-set of the West, the insistence on Eternity, the obsession with unity and coherence, the demands for predictability and justice in a world that is neither predictable or just. To do away with God, Nietzsche argues, we would have to do away with (Indo-European) grammar. But more urgent, and more readily possible, is to rid ourselves of the pathologies of guilt and sin. Spirituality does not mean sacrificing one's soul to the "other-worldly."

Outline

I. Nietzsche said "God is Dead."

    A. This has deep implications, and not only for religion.

        1. God provides the foundation of morality (the Ten Commandments). He provides and sanctions moral rules and He punishes those who transgress them.

        2. God serves as a "Postulate" of Morality (Kant).

        3. God serves as the foundation for truth and rationality. Could there be any knowledge at all if there were no God?

    B. The notion of God, Nietzsche tells us, is built right into Indo-European grammar.

        1. Language shapes our view of the world, our metaphysics.

        2. Language shapes our notion of science and truth.

    C. God provides the organization of society.

        1. The organization of society is based on a self and social identity.

        2. Our sense of self and our social identities are predicated on our relation to God.

II. Nietzsche never escapes his Lutheran upbringing and some basic themes of the Lutheran religion.

    A. He sees the need for a new myth to replace Christianity.

B. He often uses images from Luther.

  1. For example, Nietzsche's "philosophizing with a hammer" draws on Luther's interpretation of the reference in Jeremiah to God's hammer, which creates by means of destroying.

  2. Nietzsche's notion of masks also derives from Luther, who speaks of God's masks.

  3. Nietzsche's talk of affirmation in terms of "Yes-saying" reflects Luther's description of the "Yes" that wells up when grace enters the sinner's soul after pride is crushed, and despair has resulted.

  4. Nietzsche borrows and secularizes Luther's image of "overflow," which Luther employed to describe the manner in which good works emanate from the soul filled with grace.

C. Nietzsche rejected Christianity, but he also accepted it as a necessary step in human evolution. It served an important historical function.

  1. Nietzsche praised the spirituality of Christianity.

  2. He saw the original teaching of Jesus as having been perverted by the Church.

III. Nietzsche declared war on the concepts of guilt and sin.

  A. Like Freud, he finds guilt and sin psychologically debilitating.

  1. Guilt is a metaphysical blemish: we all have blemished souls. Nietzsche rejects the idea that human beings are intrinsically blemished or flawed, or that we are guilty.

  2. Nietzsche views "sins" as the foibles that make human beings interesting. For example, the seven deadly sins are manifestations of natural human instincts.

  3. It is outrageous to speak of these as metaphysical faults. They are simply part of human behavior.

  B. Accordingly, guilt and sin are metaphysically dubious and theologically contemptible.

  C. Nietzsche did retain the notion of conscience.

  1. Nietzsche did not give up spirituality but transformed it.

  2. Nietzsche wants to return us to a state of innocence, as opposed to guilt.

3. He wants to return us to self-esteem, after science has shown us that we are not the center of the universe or the pinnacle of nature.
4. Nietzsche calls for a spirituality of this world.

Essential Reading:

R. J. Hollingdale, ed., *A Nietzsche Reader*, "Religion," pp. 167–193.

Supplemental Reading:

Martin Heidegger, "Nietzsche as Metaphysician" in Robert C. Solomon, ed., *Nietzsche*, pp. 105–113.

Walter Kaufmann, "The Death of God and the Revaluation" in Robert C. Solomon, ed., *Nietzsche*, pp. 9–28.

J. Salaquarda, "Nietzsche and the Judeo-Christian Tradition" in *Cambridge Companion*, pp. 90–118.

Questions to Consider:

1. What does it mean to say, "God is dead"?
2. In what sense does Nietzsche continue to be a "spiritual" person?

Lecture Four—Transcript
"God Is Dead"—Nietzsche and Christianity

Solomon: In his book, *The Gay Science*, Nietzsche famously writes, in a section called "The Madman," "Have you not heard of that madman who lit a lantern in the bright morning hours, ran to the marketplace, and cried incessantly, 'I see God, I see God'? As many of those who did not believe in God were standing around just then, he provoked much laughter. 'Has he got lost?' asked one. 'Did he lose his way like a child?' asked another, 'or is he hiding? Is he afraid of us? Has he gone on a voyage, perhaps emigrated?' Thus they yelled and laughed. The madman jumped into their midst and pierced them with his eyes. 'Whither is God?' he cried. 'I will tell you! We have killed him, you and I. All of us are his murderers.'" Then a bit later, "'I have come too early,' the madman said, 'My time is not yet. This tremendous event is still on its way, still wandering. It has not yet reached the ears of men.'"

The fact that Nietzsche is an atheist comes as a surprise to no one. He takes his atheism very seriously. In a book of about the same period, written just a year or so before, he writes, "Historical refutation is the definitive refutation. In former times, one sought to prove that there is no God. Today, one indicates how the belief that there is a God could arise and how this belief acquired its weight and importance. A counterproof that there is no God thereby comes superfluous. In former times atheists did not know how to make a clean sweep." That's pretty definitive, and of course the idea that one should explain belief in God—How such a belief should have arisen rather than, as theologians have often tried to do, to justify or prove the existence of God—that, of course, is perfectly in line with Nietzsche's general attitude towards psychology and the idea of explaining philosophical ideas rather than justifying them.

But I think it is very important not to take Nietzsche's attack on God or his thesis, famously stated as "God is dead," as simply a kind of theological or anti-theological slogan. Rather, it has profound implications, as Nietzsche indicates here, and it's not just about theology. It's not just about religion at all. For example, for a long time, arguably since the Old Testament, morality has been thought to rest on a foundation with God as that foundation. It is, as Ivan Karamazov says, "If there is no God, everything is permitted," the idea being that it is God who provides us with the rules. It is God who sanctions the rules. It is for God's sake or out of fear of punishment by God that we obey the rules. The idea is that without God there would be no morality and no reason for being moral.

Even someone like Immanuel Kant, who argues, as I suggested in another lecture, that morality should be considered as a matter of reason, ultimately he wants to say that morality and religion are intimately tied together. As he puts it, "Belief in God is a postulate, a kind of corollary, a necessary entailment of belief and morality." So if we abandon our belief in God, if we no longer believe what we once believed, would we still say we believe and believe it in our hearts, not just in terms of some routine slogans? Somebody asks you, "Do you believe in God?" You say, "Yes." That's not the point. But you look around and see, Do people really believe in this? The answer, Nietzsche says, is "no." If that's true, then we should expect that they are quickly going to lose their faith in morality as well, and he predicts a fairly horrendous twentieth century in which the belief in God and the belief in morality have disintegrated, but it goes deeper than that.

There is a sense in which belief in God lies at the very heart of our thinking. I have sometimes thought, "How much of philosophy in the last 2,000 years really is the product of theology—thinking about God as in some sense the foundation, the unity of all things, the creator, and we are all creations?" And Nietzsche sees that this belief, this idea of there being a unity, a substance, an underlying foundation—whereas it's present in earlier Greek philosophy—nevertheless is fundamental and absolutely pervasive in Christian thinking, and not just in Christian thinking because what we find is that, for example, our grammar reflects a kind of syntax: subject, object, something is the base, something else is the property, which Nietzsche says is very much at the basis of religion and at the basis of metaphysics and at the basis of a good many of our beliefs.

One could talk about other religions here, too, of course. In ancient Hinduism, the notion of Brahmin, the one unity, the real substance of which everything else is just a manifestation, comes to mind. But the general idea is that belief in God is not just about religion; it's not just about theology. Belief in God really structures the way we think about the world. And, as we will see in a later lecture, such notions as the notion of truth, quite the contrary of being ultimately a scientific notion, ultimately has to be traced back to such theological origins. Nietzsche says, in one of his most telling comments, that we should not be rid of God until we get rid of grammar. The idea is that God is so basic to our thinking that there is a sense in which Godlike thinking, whether or not you are a theist or an atheist, is going to permeate everything that you think, and much of what Nietzsche wants to do is to somehow change that perspective.

Finally, one can point out that, for Nietzsche, God organizes society. This is obviously true in the Catholic Church, and, for many, many centuries, of course, there was no real distinction between secular power and religious authority. But even though, with the Reformation, with the Enlightenment, with modern political thinking, we have gotten away from that particular wedding, there is still a sense in which we think about society, we think about politics in the same kind of hierarchical terms with someone of absolute authority at the top that was so obvious and straightforward in the Catholic Church. And what Nietzsche wants to say as well is that, if there is a new politics—and, as I said, Nietzsche is not particularly a political thinker—but if there is a new politics, it, too, has to get rid of the image of the political body on the model of Christianity.

Higgins: Besides God being the basis for the organization of society, I think it's fair to say that God is the basis for a lot of the organization of Nietzsche's thought. Although Nietzsche is probably not so well-known as a religious thinker, as a kind of quasi-political one, or a cultural rabble-rouser, nevertheless, I think it's quite reasonable to say that he is a religious thinker. He is concerned, and this is evident in the passage Bob read, with the fact that the society he lives in has become largely a secular society. It hasn't come to grips with that. In fact, many of the people who are contributing the most to its secular way of looking at the world aren't really aware of what they have left out of the story, any kind of mythic basis for reality.

In his talk about Christianity, I think Nietzsche is very often very consciously attempting to suggest the need for a new myth. When he says that God is dead, he is not simply saying that people no longer believe in God, something that many people already know, despite what the madman says. Instead, he is pointing out that there is a complete absence of a foundational myth. One of the many strategic ways in which Nietzsche pursues this line of thought is to suggest that, after all, we do need a new myth, and he draws attention to this by utilizing some of the phraseology that's well-known from his own tradition. He quotes or paraphrases Scripture in many a passage. For example, in the madman discussion, the madman at one point says, they have done it themselves and yet they know not what they do. Anyone familiar with the New Testament will probably recognize that as not much of a change, even in wording, from what Christ says on the cross: "Father forgive them; they know not what they do."

What I am going to draw attention to for a minute is the way in which Nietzsche also utilizes a lot of phrases from a more recent religious thinker, Martin Luther, the central figure in his own immediate background, because I think a lot of those images are images that are very much misunderstood in Nietzsche. Most people reading them don't recognize that there is a kind of religious base and that Nietzsche is using these to call attention to the need to develop a new kind of basis for answering spiritual questions, if not the Christian God then at least something that serves much the same purpose.

One of the most well known phrases in Nietzsche is his idea of philosophizing with a hammer, and certainly this connotes a lot of violence. What I think escapes notice oftentimes is the fact that this was a particular line from actually the Old Testament or the Hebrew Bible that Luther had particular fondness for and discussed at great length. The line in question is from Jeremiah: "My word is a hammer, which breaks the rock in pieces," and one of Luther's comments about it is, "God wounds in order to heal." Now, why do I think that this is importantly in the background of what Nietzsche has to say? One of his ways of parsing the whole notion of a hammer is to talk about how the hammer actually is used to, as he puts it, sound out idols, to see when idols have become hollow, and that is precisely what he wants to do with the Christian God.

In this, he is following a tradition that also, besides the ones that Bob referred to in the last lecture, follows the thought of Ludwig Feuerbach. Feuerbach was famous for suggesting that humanity was not the creation of God; by contrast, humanity created God, and one of the unfortunate side effects of this was that the more humanity developed its religious thought about God, the more of its own positive powers, its positive virtues it relegated to God, thereby diminishing humanity's sense of self and awareness of its own powers. So, rather than say that one did something out of one's own virtue, the tendency was to attribute this to God. God provided grace. Anything negative that happened tended to be human responsibility, but anything virtuous couldn't really be taken as part of oneself.

So what Nietzsche sees as a positive potential of sounding out the most famous idol, namely, the idol of the Christian God, is for us to realize, after all, that the whole story of the Christian God was a human invention and, in fact, its very greatness, its power to synthesize society for so long, was a human production. If we could achieve that kind of great basis for thought at one point, surely we have the resources to come up with an alternative myth.

But back to the hammer. Another feature of this hammer image, besides sounding out idols to see which are hollow, is actually to take the hammer and smash those idols that don't end up really providing anything useful to humanity anymore. This sort of violent image is one that comes directly from both the Old Testament and Luther's gloss on it, the idea that there is an attempt to create, but to create only by means of destroying, and that's something that Nietzsche wants to suggest that humanity needs to do. So, again, there is a sense of a role that used to be played by God. God wounding in order to heal is now something that we, in the aftermath of the death of God, might take seriously in doing ourselves. What we ought to do is try to recreate, but we can only do that first by destroying.

Another frequently mentioned image in Nietzsche that I think stems in many ways from Luther is the notion of masks. Bob's already drawn attention to Nietzsche's own mask, that of a mustache, but Nietzsche frequently talks about how so much of perceived human behavior really masks the actual motive, and again I think there is a kind of reference to Luther's discussion of God wearing many masks. We can't always see God's motives. Instead, we see masks of God. If Nietzsche wants to put humanity in the place formerly occupied by humanity's own invention, namely God, what he wants to do is draw attention to the fact that we ourselves in our own motives are filled with masks. Again, it's kind of putting humanity in the place of the object of most interest and eliminating God from that position since, practically, we have already done that.

One of Nietzsche's particular emphases throughout his philosophy that we will be talking about a lot in this series is his talk of affirmation, of saying yes to life, to one's own life, specifically, and, again, I think that there is a kind of reference back to Luther using this kind of terminology. For example, Luther discussing the way in which God effuses grace into the soul involves a rather elaborate scenario in which the pride of the sinner first of all has to be crushed, indeed, by a hammer in some locutions, and, after that pride is crushed, despair will descend. At this moment of despair, the sinner is finally open for God's grace to come in, and one of Luther's own lines about this is, "Deeper than no and above it, the deep mysterious yes." Nietzsche's many oppositions of yes saying to life and saying no, I think, draws again very directly from this image, that what he wants to put in place of a kind of negative orientation that he himself thinks is a necessary stage to pass through is ultimately to look for this position from which we can say yes to life, to appreciate it fully.

A final Lutheran image or image that precedes Luther but that Luther draws a lot of attention to is the idea of overflow. Nietzsche often talks about the person that's really full of vitality and life and the desirability of living in such a way that one's own spirit flows over, that it becomes evident in everything that one does. That sense of affirmation about life is not something that just is content to sit with itself but involves a lot of interaction. Health becomes dynamic, and this is precisely the sort of thing that Nietzsche sees already in Luther when he talks about the person who really has Christian faith performing good works out of a kind of overflow—so filled with God's grace this grace overflows in good works. Nietzsche wants to borrow that image but secularize it and say, indeed, it isn't God's grace but our own power that overflows.

Certainly, he does have many harsh things to say about Christianity, and we will discuss some more. Already we have alluded to some of them. He thinks too many people are mindlessly conformist in external observance without really thinking through exactly what their true motives actually are, and he is very much on the alert for what he sees as a kind of self-righteous hypocrisy that masks itself in Christian locutions. He himself uses masks of Christian locutions but tries not to be so hypocritical about them. Even so, he thinks that Christianity has served a really important historical function for people, and I think it's very interesting that, in the passage about the madman, it's not people who believe in God that the madman assaults.

The madman assaults those people who think they can just eliminate the need that God once filled in society for something like God, who think that, by focusing all attention on science, they can simply eliminate myth and ignore the needs of humanity that have led humanity up to this point. Nietzsche thinks that is very ungrateful but the way in which we should show our greatest gratitude to this kind of thought of humanity is to think beyond it.

Solomon: There is a sense, of course, in which Nietzsche rejects Christianity wholesale, and there are two concepts in particular that Nietzsche says he just wants to get rid of, and those are the concepts of guilt and sin. Now guilt, of course, has taken quite a beating since Nietzsche and Freud got ahold of it and declared it, if not always, certainly often, a neurotic symptom, that guilt is something pathological, but, for Nietzsche, it's even worse. Guilt is metaphysical; so is sin. So, by the way, is the concept of evil, which ties them together, which is to say it's not just a function of human projection, and it's not just a function of human valuation, but, as it's perceived, guilt and sin are both something else. They are essential features of the world. Guilt, in particular is metaphysical in the fact that it is a property or an acquired property of the soul.

One of my Catholic friends, as a young girl, was told in school that she had to paint a picture of her soul, and the picture of the soul consisted of taking a black crayon and making appropriate smudges, which represented her sins. It's the notion of guilt as a metaphysical blemish and, of course, together with the doctrine of original sin, what it says is we all have blemished souls. Now Nietzsche doesn't believe in that kind of a soul, although he is certainly not soulless, but he certainly wants to say that picture of the basic blemish, that idea that somehow we are fallen, the very idea that we are initially, from the outset, somehow failed or flawed creatures, is something we should not accept.

That's not to say that Nietzsche thinks we are perfect; quite the opposite. He is all in favor of making more of ourselves, of the need to struggle to become who we are, but, nevertheless, this idea of a metaphysical anchor that prevents that—the idea that we are essentially guilty in some fundamental way—is something he utterly rejects. And, in line with Nietzsche's general attitude towards life, one can anticipate he has the same attitude towards sin. In fact, when you think about sin in the Christian tradition, something very odd should strike you: that the most serious crimes—murder, theft, treachery, rape—aren't the things that are talked about the most, partly, of course, because the wrongness of them is taken for granted. But if you think, for example, of the list of so-called "seven deadly sins," I think you get a real insight into what's going on here.

In fact, these are human foibles; they are features of the human circus. They are things that make us amusing, things that make us sometimes silly, but, nevertheless, it's what defines many of our characters. Run down the list. Lust—there is something very strange about the attack on lust in, for example, St. Paul. It's not as if lust is something to be overcome. Nietzsche's Dionysian temperament says quite clearly, lust is something to be enjoyed but, of course, in a way that is appropriate and suitable. Or gluttony—now, I don't know what your attitude towards food is, but drawing again from Feuerbach, we might say that gluttony is something that is essentially human. A certain amount of discipline, self-control, politeness, if you like, is certainly necessary, but, nevertheless, gluttony isn't a sin, much less a deadly sin. Gluttony is just a feature of being human.

Greed—well, perhaps that's more exaggerated in the twentieth century than it was before the sort of outset of global capitalism. Nevertheless, greed has always been with us, and there is a sense in which greed is not necessarily evil. To be sure, sometimes it causes great harm, but, in most people, greed is just one of those little things about them, something to joke about, something to criticize them about, something to gossip about, but, again, it's part of the human circus. Anger—can you imagine a world without anger? Aristotle, I think very insightful on these matters, talks about anger not as a sin, but, quite to the contrary, as something that the good person will naturally feel in the right kind of circumstances. Not to get angry in the appropriate circumstances to the appropriate degree at the appropriate person, he says, is to be a fool. So to think of anger as a sin right away makes you think something very deep and something very different from what is being pronounced here is actually going on.

Envy, well, I hate to say it, but envy is a basic human emotion, and for someone who sees human behavior as really basically competitive, envy quite naturally is going to be an inevitable outcome. Nietzsche talks at great length, of course, about envy's twin sister, and that is resentment, which he says explains an awful lot about human behavior and Judeo-Christian morality in particular. Then there is pride. What's so bad about pride?

Again, let me refer back to Aristotle. What Aristotle points out is that pride is nothing but what we would call, in rather California-ish terms, self-esteem, thinking well of oneself, recognizing one's accomplishments and exploits. But, of course, in Christian theology, pride is considered a sin, and, in fact, on some of the lists, pride is the number one sin because it's paying attention to yourself instead of to God.

And finally the odd sin of the seven, sloth. But is sloth really a sin? I mean, should you be sent to prison for it, should you be damned for it? The truth is that human laziness is another butt of jokes and gossip. It may not be a recipe for success in this rather hurly-burly ambitious world, but, nevertheless, I think most of us could use a good dose of sloth in our lives. And the truth is to talk about these as sins—to talk about these as metaphysical failures of some sort—is really to say something outrageous. What Nietzsche wants to do in his war on guilt and sin is to say, in effect, "Look, guilt as it's conceived—not as a matter of responsibility, and not as simply a matter of shame, which is a different matter, too—but guilt as it's conceived as a kind of embarrassment before God, as something that's essentially flawed about you, is something that must be overcome and rejected, and the notion of sin or evil as a kind of metaphysical writ, rather than simply part of the human circus, part of human behavior is something we have to overcome, too."

Now, just to anticipate, that's not to say that Nietzsche doesn't recognize the existence of profound evil in the sense that we would all accept. What he rejects and what he attacks is the notion of evil as it's attached to metaphysics, as it's attached to theology, as a set of absolute values, and, in some of his most challenging statements, what he says is, in effect, that insofar as one is interested in, for example, the preservation and happiness of the human race, it has been more advanced at some points in history by profound evil than it has been by anything else, and, of course, he has some controversial examples. He uses Caesar, Napoleon; I am sure if he had lived to be much older he would not have used Hitler, although one can even argue there, to be very polemical, that much of the morality of the late twentieth century has, in fact, been defined by the Holocaust, and we would not now have war crimes tribunals for crimes against humanity if it weren't for that horrible occasion in human history.

©1999 The Teaching Company.

So the basic idea is to take in the big picture, to ask what human beings are really like, whether human beings really need this religious foundation and this kind of absolutism in their morals, and Nietzsche's answer is a very general, strong "no."

Higgins: In general, I think that one way you can describe Nietzsche's attack on Christianity is that what he wants to do is return us to innocence. In fact, he talks about the innocence of the senses, the idea of nature as something that he hopes someday we will again be able to see innocently and the idea that its basic instincts are attacked in listing the various actions or attitudes that fall into the categories of the seven deadly sins. All of those, I think Nietzsche would say, indicate that we are really not innocent about ourselves any longer. You might say that his overall spiritual goal is to return us to a kind of self-esteem, a kind of self-esteem that's lost when humanity has put all of its own virtues into a conception of God, a conception of God that sees all and mostly notes faults in humanity.

One other feature of this I think is important as well and very timely for Nietzsche—Nietzsche is writing after people have, in a sense, come to grips with the idea that the earth is no longer the center of the universe; it's not even the center of the solar system. In fact, it's a pretty undistinguished planet, and our sun is a fairly undistinguished sun. In a sense, we have lost all moorings from an earlier tradition in the West, a tradition that was infused with the notion of the human place in the scheme of things and God having made humanity at a certain pinnacle. All that has been lost as science has developed more and more understanding of our natural place in the scheme of things. Couple that with the loss of God, the loss of self-esteem as having this premier place in nature—Nietzsche thinks that it's absolutely essential for humanity to gain some kind of sense of its own importance. Thus, what he calls for is a spirituality of this world that recognizes our own virtues as virtues and recognizes the world we live in as beautiful.

Thank you.

Lecture Five
Nietzsche and the Greeks

Scope:

Nietzsche was obsessed with the ancient Greeks. He discovered them as a schoolboy and they remained his ideal throughout his life. His last crazed note was signed "Dionysus." In this fascination, Nietzsche displayed what E. Butler has called "the tyranny of Greece over Germany." Nietzsche loved the ancient tragic playwrights Aeschylus and Sophocles, but he (very unfairly) despised their younger colleague Euripides. He displayed great admiration for the pre-Socratic philosopher Heraclitus, but expressed contempt for the great philosophers Socrates and Plato. But he envied Socrates too.

Outline

I. Nietzsche's obsession with the ancients was widespread in educated Germany ("the tyranny of Greece over Germany").

   A. Nietzsche was a brilliant philologist.
   1. He viewed Greece as a model for life and not merely as antiquity.
   2. Nietzsche despised most of his fellow scholars ("scholarly oxen") and sharply contrasted them with the people they studied.
   3. Nietzsche took Homer as his focus and the Homeric warriors as his heroes. The Bronze Age, rather than the age of Socrates, was his focus.
   4. The Greeks viewed tragedy very differently than modern people do, and this can be seen in Greek tragedy (e.g., *Oedipus the King, Antigone*).

II. Nietzsche's first published work (1872) was *The Birth of Tragedy*.

   A. The book concerned the origins and nature of Greek tragedy. It also contained a philosophy of life.
   1. The Greeks are contrasted with Christians.
   2. Philosophy is juxtaposed against the Greek view of tragedy.
   B. Greek tragedy involved the dialectical opposition of opposing principles, the Apollonian and the Dionysian.

1. The Apollonian presents the world as orderly, with definite boundaries. It suggests a sense of self as an individuated ego.
2. The Dionysian presents the world as dynamic and chaotic. It undercuts the impression that one exists as a separate individual and suggests a sense of self as part of the dynamic whole.

C. Greek tragedy became possible when two vital forces became integrated; e.g., the wild ecstasies of the Dionysian cults and rational thinking as represented by the God Apollo.
   1. The Apollonian presents the world as orderly, with definite boundaries. It suggests a sense of self as an individuated ego.
   2. The Dionysian presents the world as dynamic and chaotic. It undercuts the impression that one exists as a separate individual and suggests a sense of self as part of the dynamic whole.
   3. The best examples of this fusion of opposites were the dramas of Aeschylus and Sophocles.

D. Nietzsche conceived of Greece as an *agonistic* society.
   1. It flourished through competition.
   2. It rejected the claim that people are equal. Life consisted of winners and losers.
   3. Nietzsche thought this agonistic perspective was what made the Greeks beautiful (if also what ultimately caused them to decline).

E. Nietzsche condemned Euripides as causing the demise of Greek tragedy.
   1. He (Euripides) fell under the spell of Socrates, who wanted rational explanation of everything.
   2. Sophocles, by contrast, had seen life as a mystery.
   3. In Euripides, the rational, Apollonian side took full control. Tragedy was "rationalized," and the tragic sense of life came to an end.
   4. According to Nietzsche, Socrates hated life and saw it as something to be overcome.
   5. Nietzsche thought that life should be accepted and enjoyed for exactly what it is.
   6. His interest in the myth of eternal recurrence reflects his sense that life should be appreciated for its own sake.

III. Nietzsche did not see Greek philosophy as a great step forward for mankind. Rather, he saw it as a decline and a loss of nerve.

   A. The philosopher whom Nietzsche most admired was the Pre-Socratic Heraclitus, the philosopher of "flux," the sage with the "dark sayings."

   B. By contrast, the pre-Socratic Parmenides, Socrates and his student Plato appealed to an eternal reality and downgraded ordinary experience.

      1. Zeno, for example, even claimed that movement is an illusion.

      2. Plato's ideal world was another world, a world without change. Plato's "Myth of the Cave" suggests this.

   C. Nietzsche saw Socrates in particular as a problem, as the man who made "reason into a tyrant." But he also saw him as something of a role model, and viewed him with a mixture of love, loathing and envy.

Essential Reading:

"Homer's Contest," "Philosophy in the Tragic Age of the Greeks," and *Birth of Tragedy* in Schacht, ed., *Nietzsche: Selections.*

Nietzsche, *Twilight of the Idols*, "The Problem of Socrates."

Supplemental Reading:

Robert John Ackermann, *Nietzsche*, Chapter 1.

Walter Kaufmann, *Nietzsche*, "Nietzsche's Attitude toward Socrates."

Alexander Nehamas, *The Art of Living*, Chapter 5.

Questions to Consider:

1. Why were the ancient Greeks so appealing to the Germans, especially to Nietzsche ?

2. In what sense is Socrates a "decadent," according to Nietzsche?

Lecture Five—Transcript
Nietzsche and the Greeks

Nietzsche was obsessed with the Greeks. He discovered them as a schoolboy, and one can only imagine the fantasies he must have had as a very young man. They stayed with him throughout his life. In fact, his last crazed note, well into his period of insanity, he signed Dionysus. There's a contrast that goes throughout his philosophy between the ancient Greeks and modern bourgeois Christianity, and there is a sense in which understanding what he liked about the Greeks, or what he loved about the Greeks, is essential to understanding what he disliked and sometimes what he despised about modern society.

He was, of course, a philologist—that means a classics professor. He knew his ancient texts very well. The Greece that he really admired, though, was not the Greece that you would expect him, as a philosopher, to have loved. He thinks that the Greece of Socrates and Plato and Aristotle was already in some sense decadent. The Greece that Nietzsche really praised and admired was the Greece of Homer, the Greece of the ancient tragedians, the Greece of tragedy, and his first book, *The Birth of Tragedy*, talks at great length about the ways in which tragedy became possible for the Greeks and, consequently, the ways in which tragedy has become unthinkable for us now.

The obsession with the ancients was not Nietzsche's alone. Germany in general was taken with the Greeks. There was a growing awareness, for one thing, that Germany—and it was not yet fully Germany—but Germany was aware of the fact that it was increasingly a backward country compared with France, compared with England, and, consequently, he was very defensive. If one traces the history of the nineteenth century, what one traces is a coming to awareness of German culture, a kind of defensiveness that German culture really does deserve the same place in the sun as, say, French culture or English philosophy. By the time we get to Nietzsche, of course, we've got a unified Germany under Bismarck, but, nevertheless, there is still a profound defensiveness about it, and Nietzsche is very keenly aware of this as opposed, he thinks, to ancient Greece.

The influence of the Greeks was so profound, not just on Nietzsche but on the German cultural elite in general, that Butler a few years ago wrote a book called *The Tyranny of Greece over Germany*. It's a very apt title. There is a sense in which, since the eighteenth century, the Germans had looked to Greece as a kind of golden age, the time when human life was, if not perfect, as good as it gets, and the modern period, by contrast, is inferior, maybe pathetic. Nietzsche thinks it's very important, though, not to simply dismiss modernity because, as I said, when he wrote in a very early essay about history, he made the point that simply getting lost in history, simply bemoaning the fact, as some of his predecessors had done, that Greece was so wonderful and we're so impoverished, leads to a really lousy life.

So, the important thing is Greece should be a kind of model, and he despised his fellow scholars. I'll leave it open to what extent this might still apply today. He called them "scholarly oxen" who worried about Greek grammar, who worried about Greek philology, who worried about when such and such was written or performed but didn't spend even a minute fantasizing about what it would be like to live as a Greek and, in particular, what it would be like to live as a Greek, a Greek German, today. The Greece that he admired is very much the Greece of Homer, or, more accurately, since Homer is writing about other events or talking about other events really four centuries earlier, it's the Greece depicted by Homer, and, of course, this gives rise to one of those rumors we had talked about that Nietzsche really liked barbarians. It's hard to think about Achilles and Agamemnon and Menelaus and the gang without thinking of those barbarians; they were. Nevertheless, there is a sense in which the virtues they displayed, the attitude towards life was something that was enviable and was clearly something missing in the modern world.

If you think about the tragedies that were written by the great Greek playwrights (this is all before Socrates)—plays like *Oedipus*, *Antigone*, the plays about the Trojan women, *Prometheus*, what you realize is that it's a model of life that we have trouble understanding. It's so cruel. It's so stark—I mean, the idea of a fate driving Oedipus to do these awful things, a curse that had been cast on his father, now extending to him, which, of course, would extend in turn to his daughter Antigone. The idea of realizing that one had done something pretty awful, murdering your father, marrying your mother, and consequently putting your own eyes out because you had seen too much. That kind of vision to us is just plain awful, and so one of the themes of *The Birth of Tragedy* is how it was different for the Greeks, and how, when they saw these tragedies performed, something very different was going on.

In fact, the theme of *The Birth of Tragedy*, at its very core, is that tragedy is a real, honest recognition of what life is all about. To be sure, Oedipus, Antigone—these are people that faced dilemmas, situations that none of us really would like to face, but the truth of it is, of course, we all are going to face our own dilemmas. We all have to face up to death. We all have to face up to the bad things in life, and the question is, How do we do that? Do we accept it as the way things are, or do we rationalize it away? The idea in *The Birth of Tragedy*, which we'll talk about in much more detail in the next lecture, is that the Greek view of tragedy was possible because two different strains of thought or two different strains of feeling came together in a remarkable way.

The one, the Apollonian, the rationalistic, saw tragedy as something that happens to the individual. It's a real, personal loss. On the other hand—and what I'd like to emphasize here is the Dionysian, and the Dionysian is connected up with what you might you call the suprapersonal—it's the idea of ourselves as part of the flow of life, and if you think about orgiastic rituals, if you think about what Hegel called bacchanalian revels, one of the things that's most pronounced about it is a loss of the sense of self, a sense of going with the flow, a sense that one is part of life and that what happens to one as an individual really is of no great importance. That sense of overriding passion of identity with the whole as opposed to a kind of rational individualism is what Nietzsche thinks allows the Greeks to come up with this notion: on the one hand, something awful happening to an individual; at the same time, understanding this as something beautiful.

The Birth of Tragedy makes a distinction, however, between two different sets of Greek authors. Nietzsche sees the early great tragedians, namely Sophocles and Aeschylus, as very much in tune with this merging of the Apollonian and the Dionysian, getting the two in balance, whereas the third of the great three Greek tragedy writers, Euripides, Nietzsche really condemns. He condemns him in particular because of his linkage—which is debatable in classical circles—but his linkage with Socrates in particular. With Euripides and with Socrates, that's when Greek thought and Greek culture goes into decline. The difference was that Sophocles and Aeschylus saw tragedy as something that's inexplicable, something that could be rationalized. You watch *Oedipus* or *Antigone*, both plays by Sophocles, and the overwhelming sense you come away with, apart from the beautiful poetry, is that life is really a mystery, that the things that happen to people can't be explained.

With Euripides, on the other hand, what Nietzsche says, anyway, is rationalization enters the picture, and, of course—whether or not the link with Socrates can be ultimately sustained—that Euripides and Socrates in common tried to explain tragedy in such a way that human beings could ultimately think their way through it, and that's precisely what Nietzsche wants to say one could not do. He also thinks that the ancient Greeks had, as one of their primary virtues, the fact that they were agonistic, the fact that they believed in struggle, that life itself was a struggle. The tragedies make this very clear, and, of course, Homer's two great books, the *Iliad* and the *Odyssey*, make it amply clear to what extent life is always a struggle of one sort or another. In the more peaceful version of this struggle, the Olympics—which come, after all, from ancient Greece—there is an illustration of the way in which this sense of ferocious competition is something that goes all the way back to the Greeks.

Despite our pretensions, at least until a few years ago, that the Olympics are rather amateurish—if you like, a kind of genteel sporting event—with the Greeks, it was very clear that it was more than that. This cut right to the quick of human nature. It wasn't just sport; it was life. This sense of agone, this sense of struggle, was, Nietzsche thought, what made the Greeks so beautiful, and that's the word he uses over and over again—that they saw life in terms of a struggle, and the struggle itself became an artistic form. The idea of looking at life as a struggle even extends to such supposedly genteel professions as philosophy. One often talks about Socrates in terms of his love of the truth, his pursuit of wisdom, and certainly that's how he talked about himself, but you don't have to read much of Plato to see right through that.

What Socrates really loves is a good argument. What he really likes is to get down and dirty in the streets and show that he is the smartest guy of all. Socrates is as competitive as any philosopher has ever been, and, in fact, one might argue that Socrates sort of set the model for what philosophers think of themselves today. The important thing is winning arguments. Socrates is often contrasted with the Sophists, a school of philosophers who were pretty much his contemporaries. I sometimes think of them as the ancient equivalent of law school because in democratic Greece their function was to teach people the art of rhetoric, to teach them how to make arguments, to teach them how to win arguments, and Socrates contrasts himself on the grounds that that's all they do. What he is about, on the other hand, is the truth.

But, as several of my classes and friends have argued in great detail, I think the truth is that Socrates wasn't against the Sophists so much as he was one of them. In fact, he was the best of them. That agonistic sense—life as struggle, life as tension—extended even to philosophy. What Socrates *says* in philosophy—quite to the contrary. The idea of Greece's agonistic also explains, in Nietzsche's terms, why Greece declined. In the early days of Greece, when there were constant wars between the city-states, invasions from the Persians, and so on, there was always the struggle, and Nietzsche says—and this is one of the places where he stretches history—"As long as the Greeks had a struggle going on they knew what life was about and they were great. As soon as they found themselves in a period of relative peace, what happened was that that kind of inner instinct for struggle turned against themselves and that's when they started to decay."

The idea of Greek tragedy as two vital forces, then, gets resolved or, shall we say, destroyed by an overemphasis by Euripides, but mainly by Socrates, on the rationalistic, on the Apollonian. In fact, one of the features of Socrates' philosophy that has often been commented on, but perhaps not in the properly unsympathetic way, is that what Socrates is all about is, in a way, a kind of denial of tragedy. He says, for example, that the only thing that a truly good man has to worry about is the status of his own soul, and, if he is properly attentive to the status of his soul, to the health of his soul, nothing else can harm him.

Now, if you think about poor Oedipus, Oedipus was a good man. Oedipus, in fact, did everything that was expected of him within the context of the culture. I think we should say Oedipus did everything that Socrates would say he ought to do, even—much to his detriment—self-examination of a very profound sort. But the idea that this somehow inoculated him, made him immune from misfortune, obviously quite the contrary was true. The truth is that bad things happen to good people. But Socrates' philosophy ultimately is that there is this thing called the eternal soul that outlives the body, that, in fact, lives forever, and Socrates had a fantasy of a more perfect world in which his pure soul could think pure ideas without the interference of all these bodily temptations, instincts, and sufferings.

As I said, I think the truth is actually the opposite. If Socrates' soul had lived on forever just thinking by itself without anyone to argue with, I think, in fact, it would have been a pretty miserable soul. Because Nietzsche is right. What makes Socrates tick is human engagement, human encounter, this kind of competitive struggle. What gives way when we abandon the Dionysian, the sense of reckless abandon in favor of the purely rationalistic, in favor of the Apollonian is that we stop thinking in terms of life because life is, after all, at least in part Dionysian. When we start thinking with Socrates that life is reason, that life is pure rationality and that understanding life, thinking beyond tragedy is possible, then there is a sense in which we deny life itself.

As I suggested, Nietzsche's argument even goes further than this. He says, for example, to understand Socrates' philosophy is to understand that Socrates actually hated life. Appearances to the contrary, as I said, Socrates is, very clearly in Plato's dialogues, a very jolly, happy soul who loves his encounters with his students and other people. He is what we would call a fulfilled human being. Nevertheless, Nietzsche points out that, on his deathbed, Socrates was executed, forced to drink hemlock for supposedly corrupting the minds of the youth and a kind of blasphemy.

But regarding when he died, Nietzsche says of him the following, "I admire the courage and wisdom of Socrates in everything he did, said, and did not say. This mocking, unenamored monster, pied piper of Athens who made the most overweening youth tremble and sob, was not only the wisest chatterer of all time, he was equally great in his silence. I wish he had remained silent at the last moment of his life, but in that case he might have belonged to a still higher level of spirits. But whether it was death, or the poison, or piety, or malice, something loosened his tongue at the last minute, and he said, 'Oh Crito [one of his friends], I owe Asclepius a rooster.'"

Asclepius was the patron saint of health, of medicine, and offering him a rooster would have been considered basically paying your doctor for curing a disease. "This ridiculous and terrible last word," Nietzsche writes, "means for those who have ears, oh Crito, life itself is a disease. Is it possible that a man like him, like Socrates, who had lived cheerfully and like a soldier in the sight of everyone, should have been a pessimist, shades of Schopenhauer? He had merely kept a cheerful demean while concealing all of his life, his ultimate judgement, his inmost feeling. Socrates! Socrates suffered life, and then he revenged himself with his veiled, gruesome, pious, blasphemous saying. Did a Socrates need such revenge? Did his over-rich virtue lack an ounce of magnanimity? Alas! My friends, we must overcome even the Greeks."

The picture there is very clear that, despite all appearances, Socrates didn't like life. Socrates saw life as something to be overcome. The fantasy that he expresses in those works, which depict his last days, that his soul might live on just doing philosophy, is a kind of liberation, and Nietzsche wants to say that's exactly the wrong picture. The right picture is accepting life for exactly what it is and enjoying it for exactly what it is. He brings up a Greek myth that we're going to come back to several times. It's a Greek myth—also, I suppose, a Persian myth—but perhaps best known as a kind of Indian myth, the myth of eternal recurrence, the idea of life circling around, coming back again.

The importance of that myth for Nietzsche, more than anything else, is the idea that life is to be emphasized for the sake of life, not for the sake of an eternal existence, not for the sake, as in Christianity, of a future heaven—that the weight of each moment is such that one should appreciate life and all the moments in life for their own sake. Now, in terms of philosophy, what Nietzsche does is, in fact, look behind Socrates. If you look before Socrates came onto the scene, and before the Sophists, there are, in fact, a whole series of Greek philosophers, and we do them the disservice of simply referring to them as the pre-Socratics, as if the first philosopher was really Socrates and these other guys that appeared first, really, well, they only barely count. They are sort of the warm-up act.

But the truth is that, well, we don't know much about them. In many cases, we don't have much of their writings, but then we can argue that we really don't have anything of Socrates' writings either because he didn't write. What we have is what we have from Plato and from Herodotus and some other Greek historians. The truth is that an awful lot was going on in Greece before Socrates, and Nietzsche, as a good philologist, was well aware of this, but again he makes distinctions. The philosopher who is clearly in a way, his favorite—the one who in many ways models his own picture of reality and picture of the universe—is Heraclitus, the philosopher who said that all is flux, everything changes. Heraclitus was the philosopher who took as his element—the primary substance of the universe—where others said it was water or air or earth, he said, "It's fire, and the important thing about fire is it's always changing. If you look at a flame, it's never the same shape twice."

For Heraclitus, struggle, strife, war was the essence of all things. The truth is that people were based on a nature that itself was always in contradiction that was always moving and changing itself. It's Heraclitus, of course, who says more or less the famous saying, "You can't step into the same river twice," the idea being that life is not something static, much less something potentially eternal. Life is something that is always changing. It is what it is, and understanding that is the real wisdom. Contrast here one of Heraclitus's contemporaries, a Greek philosopher named Parmenides, who, in many ways, anticipates much of Plato. Parmenides thought that reality is and must be, of necessity, eternal, enduring, unchanging. All of change is an illusion. The truth is that what we perceive as reality is not that at all. But, of course, because what we see is this changing world, it follows that we just don't have the capacity to know reality at all. It is and must be a mystery for us.

It's Parmenides' best-known student named Zeno who demonstrates this in a series of famous paradoxes, the idea of an arrow never reaching its mark because at each instant it's only covered half the space that it did before. Consequently, if you add up the moments—and, of course, they didn't know about infinitesimals—then the moments get smaller and smaller and smaller, but the truth is the arrow never reaches its mark. Now, of course, there is a lot to say about that. Tom Stopper perhaps did it best when he had one of those professors in a play say, "And Saint Sebastian must have died of fright."

But it seems to me that the basic idea is something much larger. It's Parmenides' philosophy, and that is, "Here is the clearest example of change—movement—but here I'm going to prove to you geometrically that movement is an illusion, that movement is impossible." What follows from this is the idea that reality has to be something else than this changing world that we perceive. This, of course, is the same philosophy that is picked up by Socrates and then most famously by Plato.

The differences and similarities between Socrates and Plato is something much debated, and this not a lecture on Greek philosophy as such, so I'm not going to try to figure out the difference. The truth is, of course, that Socrates didn't write anything. It is mainly recorded by Plato. Certainly some of the ideas were Socrates' philosophical ideas, but equally certainly much of it was embellished and, later on in his career, I think, actually just made up by Plato. So, in a way, think of Socrates and Plato in a hyphenated way, at least as far as the philosophy is concerned. And what that philosophy looks like is an emphasis on the eternal, an emphasis on the otherworldly, an emphasis on what Plato called the world of Being, a world in which there is no change, a world in which there are only perfect ideals, a world of which this world is only a shadow.

And, of course, one of Plato's most famous images, which Socrates tells in *The Republic*, is "The Myth of the Cave," in which we have a story about a bunch of prisoners chained to a cave and all that they ever see are the shadows on the wall. But suppose one of them were to turn around, break free, and actually see the world itself? It would be so dazzling that he'd probably be blinded, and if he came back and tried to tell his fellow prisoners what he had seen, they'd be so outraged that they would kill him. Of course, that's not a bad summary of what actually happened to Socrates, but it also depicts—and what Nietzsche is picking on is—the idea that this world of our experience is not the real one. There is another world, which is very different. Although Plato didn't say that this world is unreal, nevertheless, it's pretty clear that the world of our experience, the world we live in, is in some very important sense less real, less important than the world of Being. That to Nietzsche is the kind of escapism, is the ultimate refuge of, rationality, and that is why Socrates, he says, made reason into a tyrant.

Now this is something to explain in a number of different ways. Part of it, of course, might be put in straightforwardly philosophical terms, in terms of the general trend of Greek thought from the very first philosophers, and we're now talking back to, say, Hesiod the poet and Thales, who is usually credited as being the first philosopher scientist. But through Parmenides, Heraclitus is often ignored here through Socrates and Plato to Aristotle, and you look at that trend, and one way of describing it is it is the sophistication, the development, of reason. But there is another way of describing it, which is the way Nietzsche describes it, and that is it is the decline and the neglect of the Dionysian.

When I said that Nietzsche says Socrates is ugly, that he was lower class and, ultimately, that Socrates hated life, that he thought it was a disease, the main point there was to say what we find in Socrates is a need to escape, an unwillingness to accept life for what it is, the need to somehow see beyond it. And what we get, with Socrates in particular, is this emphasis on reason not just as a kind of human faculty, a human ability to think, a way of calculating, a way of manipulating concepts and so on. All that is fair enough, but reason can do something else. Reason can do what Parmenides thought it couldn't do. Reason can actually see through to the world of being, the world as it really is, and that vision, if not blinding, is so striking, Plato assures us, that, once one sees it, one will fall hopelessly and eternally in love and never be able to go back into the cave of ordinary experience.

But, of course, the other danger, the one that Nietzsche focuses on, is that what you're falling in love with also has to be reflected in terms of what you're falling out of love with. When you fall in love with reason and fall in love with this more perfect eternal world, what you do is, you fall out of love with this world and with your life, and that's what goes wrong after Greece.

Lecture Six

"Why the Greeks Were So Beautiful"— Nietzsche on Tragedy

Scope:

Nietzsche's conception of tragedy provided the famous contrast between the "Apollonian and Dionysian," between the God of light and the prince of darkness. The Apollonian and Dionysian are two aspects of Greek culture, and their synthesis explains the genius of Greek tragedy. Through tragedy, the Greeks "accepted" suffering and made something "beautiful" out of it. Christianity, by contrast, tries to deny the meaning of suffering by way of the invocation of another, better "otherwordly" life. Socrates and Plato also tried to deny the reality of suffering by beginning the long-running Western argument that there is a "reason" for everything. Aristotle's theory of tragedy presented a version of this theme. Nietzsche was anticipated, however, by Hegel and Schopenhauer.

Outline

I.   Nietzsche's conception of tragedy involved the acceptance of life as suffering.

   A. In this, he followed his pessimistic mentor Schopenhauer.

      1. He confronted Schopenhauer's pessimism by considering the Greek story of the demigod Silenus, who claimed that the best thing for a human being was not to be born; the second best, to die quickly.

      2. Schopenhauer preached withdrawing from life.

      3. The Greeks rejected withdrawal from life; they celebrated life, despite its suffering.

   B. Tragedy (for Nietzsche) is the synthesis of the Dionysian and the Apollonian.

      1. Life has to be seen from two sides.

      2. One view was from the Dionysian frenzy of life as a dynamic but integrated whole; Dionysus was associated with music and the Dionysian condition was represented by the Greek chorus.

3. The other view was from the Apollonian efforts of the individual characters (e.g., Oedipus, Antigone) to make sense of their suffering.

C. The Greeks merged the Apollonian and Dionysian ways of viewing the world.
   1. The chorus was originally the entire drama; its chanting drew the audience into the Dionysian condition of participation in something larger.
   2. Gradually actors and plot became part of Greek tragedy.
   3. But the effectiveness of the "Apollonian" spectacle depended on the audience already having been captivated by the music of the chorus.
   4. The Dionysian ideal was joy in life.
   5. Dionysus is opposed to individuality: in one account, he was torn to bits by the Titans; his devotees sought to reintegrate his severed parts, implying a reintegration of individuals into an original unity.

D. The early Greeks could accept the suffering of life.
   1. They realized that they ultimately could not rationalize tragedy.
   2. But Socrates, and then Plato and Aristotle, tried to do just that.

II. Socrates, Plato and Aristotle rationalized tragedy by focusing attention, not on this life, but on another.

A. Basically, they tried to find a safe respite from life's tragedies.
   1. Aristotle did not accept the domination of another world (*cf.* Raphael's famous painting, "The School of Athens").
   2. Aristotle, like Nietzsche, was very "this worldly"; both thought of tragedy in similar ways.

B. Finding reasons for tragedy ("why bad things happen to good people").
   1. Aristotle rationalized tragedy with his theory of the "tragic flaw."
   2. Oedipus ultimately deserved what happened to him because of his stubbornness and his arrogance. However, Oedipus was a good man; he is proud, arrogant, stubborn, but these are kingly qualities.

3. Aristotle thus allows us to rationalize tragedy by identifying a tragic flaw, which enables us to blame the victim.

C. Christianity (to Nietzsche) is the ultimate rationalization.
   1. It provides a paradigm of the "otherwordly."
   2. Nietzsche claimed that "Platonism is Christianity for the masses."
   3. Nietzsche criticized as horrendous the commonplace idea that the terrible and undeserved suffering of some individuals is part of God's plan.
   4. Unlike contemporary Christians, the Greeks did not try to rationalize away tragedy and suffering.

III. Tragedy can be viewed from a number of very different perspectives.

A. Hegel's dialectical theory views tragedy as a cosmic conflict between super-human forces, not as the consequence of a tragic flaw.
   1. Sophocles' drama *Antigone* is a good example of this view.
   2. We only make sense as a unity.
   3. We should understand tragedy, not by seeing a tragic flaw, but by seeing that people are caught in contending historical forces.

B. Schopenhauer's pessimistic view is that tragedy is an unavoidable manifestation of the irrational cosmic Will. All we can do is not take ourselves or our lives all that seriously.

C. Nietzsche rejects Schopenhauer's pessimistic view. For him, tragedy is unavoidable, but we should *love* it, nevertheless.

Recommended Reading:

Birth of Tragedy in Schacht, ed., *Nietzsche: Selections*.

Nietzsche, *Twilight of the Idols* ("What We Owe to the Ancients").

Supplemental Reading:

Ivan Soll, "Pessimism and the Tragic View of Life" in Robert C. Solomon, Kathleen M. Higgins, eds., *Reading Nietzsche*, pp. 104–131.

Julian Young, *Nietzsche's Philosophy of Art*, pp. 25–57.

Questions to Consider:

1. What is tragedy? Do we today still have a sense of what that is?

2. Is life more pain than pleasure, more suffering than gratification? How is life worth living if it necessarily ends in suffering? If it does not have an ultimate meaning?

Lecture Six—Transcript
"Why the Greeks Were So Beautiful"— Nietzsche on Tragedy

Solomon: Although Nietzsche ultimately wants to defend a philosophy that might be called "the joy of life," it is absolutely essential, from his very first works, that tragedy play a prominent part. Joy of life and tragedy are not opposites, but, rather, they are mutually necessary. What we would like to do in this lecture is to talk about the role of tragedy and the nature of tragedy in life.

Higgins: Nietzsche accomplishes really quite a lot in his first book. In a sense, he lays out an agenda that's going to continue with him throughout his entire philosophical production, and the question he asks, really, is, What was Greek tragedy all about? He ponders the fact that the Greeks seem so obsessed with these kinds of stories, tragedies, including some of the ones that Bob was taking about last time, and he ends up answering the question, pointing out that the Greeks were not only attempting a type of artistic reconciliation of opposites but actually a kind of solution to the problem of evil.

The problem of evil is a traditional religious problem. It's the problem of, could the world be good or, perhaps, could the world be the production of a good God if indeed suffering exists, and we know it does. What Nietzsche thinks the Greeks achieved in their tragedy was to provide a kind of answer that made sense to them. Actually, in raising this question, he follows his mentor, Schopenhauer, whom, as we've pointed out, thought that the world basically wasn't good, that life was essentially suffering. This, in fact, is a Buddhistic theme in Schopenhauer's thought, which we will be talking about more in the following lecture. But, at any rate, Schopenhauer's conviction was that if you look at the evil around one, the most obvious thing to do is to withdraw from life, and this is what Nietzsche thinks the Greeks were grappling with, too.

They, too, recognized that much about life, really, on the surface of it seems rather unacceptable. They had a particular myth that Nietzsche draws attention to early in *The Birth of Tragedy*—the story of a demigod named Silenus who was captured and told to answer a question. He said that he would, and the question was, "What is the best thing for man?" At this, Silenus laughed and said, "The best thing for man, after all, is not to be born at all, but the second best is to die soon." Nietzsche thought that this was, in a sense, a counterpart to the sort of philosophy that Schopenhauer had been teaching, that you really can't win in this world. The best thing to do is to be as calm as possible and live through it.

What Nietzsche sees the Greeks as doing is dealing with this question in Greek tragedy but not drawing the Schopenhauerian conclusion. Rather than concluding that what we ought to do is withdraw, tune out from life as much as we possibly can, the Greek tragedy actually showed a way of celebrating life, even despite the fact that suffering was an essential part of it.

The two principles that Bob mentioned in the previous lecture, the Dionysian and the Apollonian, as Nietzsche initially discusses them, turn out to be two artistic principles. Nietzsche considers two different kinds of art forms, both very popular in his own time, the Romantic era. One art form, that of the visual arts—and, as he sees it, particularly the art of sculpture—shows the world in a beautified form. It idealizes the appearances of things. It makes things look more beautiful than they are, but it tries to represent the world very clearly, with clear boundaries, with separate individuals, with separate entities that we can appreciate contemplatively. In this he follows both Schopenhauer and Kant in seeing beautiful images in art as a kind of way for human beings to focus on something in their world and merely enjoy them, merely enjoy contemplating them, not relating to them practically.

If you enjoy an artwork that depicts something artistically, it's not a question of seeing something in the picture that you would like to own or being motivated, for instance, if it is a still life, to want to get some food that looks as delicious as that on the painting, but, instead, ideally, when you view it as art, what you are trying to do is simply contemplate the beauty of form. By contrast, the Dionysian art that Nietzsche talks about is the art of music, and there the natural response is something quite different. Rather than simply allowing you to contemplate, music incites you to be part of something. Nietzsche points out in one of his later works, *Twilight of the Idols*, that it's actually been quite an achievement for human beings to learn to sit still in concert halls because music urges us to move, to use our whole bodies as a kind of symbolic response to this inciting element of music.

So, when the Greeks merged the two, as Nietzsche claims they do in tragedy, they are in a sense merging two very different ways of looking at the external world: one, the Apollonian way of seeing beauty, idealizing what one sees and contemplating it, taking satisfaction in it just being what it is and viewing it from a detached point of view and, by contrast, the more musical side of things, the Dionysian, which urges you to respond in as lively a way as the music itself exists. So how do these work together in Greek tragedy?

Nietzsche notes the rather interesting historical fact that the Greek tragedy actually began with the chorus alone. For most modern audiences, I think this comes as a bit of a surprise since it seems that oftentimes in productions of Greek tragedy the chorus comes on and comments on what's been going on in the play but almost seems dispensable. We tend to be following the plot, and they kind of hamper the plot's moving forward, though they comment on it, sort of urging us, maybe baiting us, to want the plot to go forward.

Nietzsche explains that, in origin, tragedy had a very, very different structure. Originally, all there was was the chorus. The chorus was essentially a group of supposed half men, half beasts—satyrs—who would come on stage and create a kind of musical stir. They would stir themselves into a kind of frenzied state, and, ideally, what would happen is that the audience would also get into this musical situation. In a sense, it was almost comparable to a rock concert, a very successful rock concert, in which the whole audience eventually feels like standing up and moving around, hopefully not too violently, in response to music that's just captivated them.

Originally, the Greek tragic performances were simply this: The satyrs would come on stage, and their poetry, and particularly their musical rendition of the poetry, would stir the audiences so much that they were in a position to actually think about the Greek myth. In a sense, the whole idea of a plot stemmed from already being in the state of mind where one could concentrate on the myth. Originally, an actor appeared on stage as a representative of the god, the god Dionysus, and when the actor appeared on stage, assuming that people actually had been captivated by the chorus, the audience didn't see simply an actor with a mask on; instead, they saw the god himself.

Nietzsche's explanation of further elaboration of Greek tragedy was simply further elaboration of stories that were consistent with the ideal of Dionysus, and we should go back again to explain exactly what this ideal was. It's a kind of sense of frenzied involvement in life, as Nietzsche describes it, particularly as its way of answering the problem of evil. It's the sense that participating in life is intrinsically pleasurable and powerful, that it simply is joyous to be alive, and that that's a much more fundamental insight than any awareness of evil, any awareness of the vulnerability we all face as individuals. So, as the audience approached the arrival of the hero, when there were actors on stage, it was already captivated by this musical state of mind. It was ready for a kind of transformation. In fact, it had already been transformed.

People walk into the theatre, and Nietzsche says, in their usual roles, judges are judges, workmen are workmen, and so on, but as soon as they become part of the audience and part of this Dionysian captivated crowd, all of these roles fall aside. They are simply part of this joyous, frenzied throng that's now capable of the true vision of the tragedy, the arrival of the god on stage. Why Dionysus represents a kind of god that's in opposition to individuality stems from a detail of the myth, at least in one of the tellings, and this story is the story of how Dionysus was ripped to pieces by the Titans and that his worshippers were always looking for a regeneration of Dionysus, his re-composition from the parts that had been torn asunder. In a sense, this was a kind of symbolic vision of what humanity is like, that human individuals seem so separate from each other, but that this is really ultimately illusory and that, despite our rather natural tendency to think of our private egos as real, the real solution to this is recognition of our oneness, our oneness through Dionysus.

So what the Greek tragic play did was allow people an insight into something about themselves. Certainly the reason that the kinds of plots that became common fare in Greek tragedy were so interesting was because they were plots about individual vulnerability. But by raising these very cases, it raised the need in the audience to somehow resolve that, and the resolution was something they were in a state of mind to be prepared for because the chorus had made them feel a kind of vitality, a vitality with the whole environment and with everyone around them. At that point, they could turn to this Dionysian resolution, namely, the arrival of the god on stage, the reminder that this separation, this vulnerability, only sees the individuated aspect of us and doesn't recognize that, in a sense, at our death, when life goes on, we go on with it.

Solomon: If the earlier Greeks did accept suffering as an inevitable part of life, in fact, as an essential aspect of life, the later Greeks and, in particular Socrates, Plato, and Aristotle, did not. I have already talked briefly about Socrates and Plato and how, in their formulation of the idea of an eternal soul, of a world that's more perfect than this one, they rationalized tragedy by saying, in effect, this suffering, this life, don't worry about it, because there is something better to come—something that clearly anticipates Christianity.

But the third member of that triad is someone I haven't talked about, and someone who, in this context, is actually extremely interesting. In fact, Aristotle has the well-deserved reputation as *the* theorist of tragedy. He didn't, as far as we know, write any tragedies, but he certainly wrote the definitive book of ancient world, *The Poetics*, in which he discusses what tragedy is, what's a good tragedy, what makes it work, and essentially lays out a whole system of rules that explain to potential playwrights the form that they should follow. What's interesting philosophically about Aristotle in this context is, first of all, that Aristotle—unlike Socrates and Plato, who was his teacher, after all—Aristotle did not accept the idea of another world.

In fact, you may know a very famous painting in the Vatican by Raphael called "The School of Athens," and inside the central arch is a depiction of Plato and Aristotle. Plato, the older man, has his finger raised towards the heavens, and Aristotle, in a very distinctive gesture, is pushing downward, emphasizing this world. So Aristotle, in one sense, is very interestingly on Nietzsche's side. In fact, one can hypothesize why Nietzsche doesn't talk more about Aristotle, who is also very similar to him in ethics, and one hypothesis is because Aristotle was still associated very much with Aquinas and Catholicism. But Aristotle himself, in addition to being very this-worldly, as Nietzsche was, also thought about tragedy in a very specific, and now well-established, way. Let me use Oedipus as an example.

One of Aristotle's theses, though by no means the major one, is that, in tragedy, although we are dealing with a noble character—a king, a queen, someone of extremely high status, typically—nevertheless, the character has a "tragic flaw," and the tragic flaw theory has been embellished in many different ways over the years. Of course, Christianity picks it up and runs with it. Original sin is one way of talking about it for everyone, but also the very notion that sins committed while you are alive can jeopardize your chance for immortal happiness—that's very much part of the same kind of thesis. In Aristotle it is more modest, but, nevertheless, it's very significant.

Take Oedipus. Oedipus, as I suggested in an earlier lecture, was a good man. If you think about the criteria for virtue, for integrity, he had it. He answered the riddle of the sphinx and he saved the city; he went on to become king. We know that he heard the myth, the rumor about himself and ran away from home, essentially to avoid harming his parents. Nevertheless, fate caught up with him, and he did so. It is Oedipus who drives the play. The play, in fact, is set during a period of pestilence in which Oedipus is trying to figure out its cause, and, even though Tiresius the seer, the sage, warns him in no uncertain but still subtle terms that he shouldn't pursue this line of questioning, Oedipus proceeds and insists until finally, of course, he discovers what the cause of the pestilence is, namely, himself and his own actions.

With this, it is often interpreted that Oedipus, in fact, is flawed. He is proud, he is arrogant, he is stubborn. Against this one can say very quickly, "He is king. Of course! That's the way kings are." As for stubbornness, isn't this just another name for what we call integrity? Now the interesting question is, Why is it so important to find this tragic flaw? And I think the answer is very revealing. Because insofar as we can watch a tragedy and we can, at a safe distance, empathize with the hero and say how terrible and feel the kind of fear and anguish that Aristotle describes, we also feel it's not going to happen to us because Oedipus is different: He is king, he is in a situation that we won't be in, he is facing a dilemma that we won't have to face, and he is flawed.

You may have noticed yourself. I find myself doing this all the time, and I hate it, and I can imagine Nietzsche having the same reaction. But there's an earthquake or a flood or some terrible tragedy somewhere in the world, and my rationalization, before I have a chance to think about it, is, "Well, it's not me, and it wouldn't be me because I am not. I am not Chinese, I am not living in the Middle East, I am not living near the San Andreas Fault, I am not living in a flood plain." Or, closer to home—"Well, the flight was Delta, I fly American." There's always the sense it is not me; I am not in the class of tragic figures.

So there is a sense in which Aristotle, in a much more subtle way, allows us to rationalize tragedy, and he does it by saying insofar as we can find something that's significantly different about the tragic figure, that's enough for us to distance ourselves and to fool ourselves into thinking that's not going to happen to me. What we do is we seek a safe respite: in Socrates and Plato, in another world; in Aristotle, in a much more sophisticated mode of rationalization. Nevertheless, the upshot of this, of course, is to try to explain tragedy, to rationalize it away, and nowhere is this more concrete and, for Nietzsche, more prone to attack than in Christianity itself.

Higgins: Of course, for Nietzsche, Christianity is, in a sense, following the model of Plato. In fact, at one point he calls it "Platonism for the masses," and what he has in mind here is the idea that what you do to explain what seems inexplicable in this world is make reference to another. So, if some tragedy befalls someone, especially someone that we don't see as particularly guilty, one of the common responses in the Christian tradition is, "God has a plan. God sees things we don't. Therefore, somehow it's rational or rationalizable. It's something we don't have to worry about; this is God's business." Not that this always cheers people up, though it's supposed to, but I think what Nietzsche sees in it is something that's even more dubious than something that fails as encouragement, namely, the fact that if you are really looking for something that rationalizes terrible things that happen to people, in a sense you are not taking the tragic feature of it seriously.

It is almost as if God is pictured as a kind of super accountant who has some kind of equation in which the correct solution comes out happening, that somehow it's worth the expense of all these people suffering in order to bring about some greater good in the end. I think Nietzsche's reaction to that is that it is appalling to think anyone would find this cheering. Indeed, this is a rather monstrous way of interpreting God's intentions, that God doesn't care about a lot of people and factors them in as part of his ultimate plan. In a sense, that makes their sufferings not really so important. They are only part of this world; they are not, in the fundamental picture, all that significant.

Nietzsche thinks the Greeks, in a sense, were facing reality more than at least much of Christian thought in resolving the problem of evil precisely because they didn't try to whitewash or eliminate the significance of real human suffering. There is a kind of willingness to just stare suffering in the face. He thought the Greeks quite reasonably thought it was important to look at what was beautiful around one as well. So one didn't dwell on the tragic all the time but, nevertheless, to acknowledge that tragedy exists, that there are some things that aren't rational and are not even rationalizable that happen to people, is simply to accept some of the conditions of life. The Greek resolution wasn't to say, "In some other plane this will all make sense." At least not the Greeks that Nietzsche viewed as heroes. Socrates and Plato, maybe, from that point of view, are not the Greeks that Nietzsche loved.

But to view this as something that can be rationalized by turning to another plane is exactly what the ancient Greeks, the pre-Socratic Greeks, didn't do. What they did instead was to say, "This is real. This is something we all face, and, nevertheless, life is so fundamentally good that we find this all worthwhile. This is well worth the price of admission for each of us. We can't make this make sense; nevertheless, we live on, and we live joyously."

Solomon: It is important not to think about tragedy just as theatre, although clearly that's part of what Nietzsche is talking about. And it is important not to think about tragedy in life as just bad things happening to good people. That happens is obvious enough, but that's really not what this discussion is about. Tragedy has a certain kind of perspective, and, for Nietzsche, it carries with it a certain sense of nobility, not necessarily that one is a king or a queen or royalty in any sense, but there is a kind of noble attitude towards life and a noble kind of acceptance. In fact, there are several ways of thinking about this, and all of it is a certain kind of perspective that has to be distinguished from the various Christian and rationalistic perspectives that we have been talking about.

One figure who plays a major role here, although Nietzsche talks surprisingly little about him—I think one has to surmise that Nietzsche really didn't know that much about him and also he was under the spell of a shadow—is Hegel, who is somebody I have mentioned before, an early, very important, nineteenth-century philosopher who had a theory of the universe, and it is one of those grand philosophical perspectives that would be worth twenty-four lectures all by itself. But the main point is that Hegel saw tragedy not as the sort of payment for a flaw, much less as something that could be overseen by appeal to another world. Hegel, although he was being interpreted at the time—and this is why I think Nietzsche didn't pay much attention to him—as a religious thinker, Hegel, in fact, was a very this-worldly thinker for whom spirituality was a this-worldly phenomenon and for whom God, insofar as one wanted to talk about God in this context at all, was not separate and different from the creation.

Hegel's theory of tragedy, consequently, is, like the early Greeks, a kind of supra-personal view that we can view ourselves as individuals, but, to do so, Hegel says, is kind of illusory. Not that he rejects it—it is an important part of modern civil society; it is an important part of our way of understanding ourselves. Nevertheless, ultimately we are all one. It's a view that Hegel certainly shares with the ancient Buddhists and Hindus, although he explicitly rejects them because he wants to appear as a Christian. It is something he shares with Schopenhauer, which is something we will talk about next time, but the view that we are all ultimately one goes straight back to the Dionysian myth and the idea that, although we think of ourselves as separate pieces, separate individuals, the truth is that we only make sense as a unity.

Nevertheless, within that unity there are very different forces. It's Hegel who makes famous the notion of dialectic; of course, it's a Greek notion. Basically, it means conversation, a back and forth, and one finds it most notably in Plato's dialogues with Socrates. But, for Hegel, dialectic is a kind of historical movement, and what defines human consciousness, what defines history, what defines the history of religion, the history of philosophy, is a kind of struggle back and forth, in other words, Nietzsche's notion of the Greek agonistic society. For Hegel, history consists of such warring forces, which, he says, with progress, with the evolution of what he calls spirit, will eventually resolve themselves into a sense of mutual or all-embracing understanding.

Within that picture, the way to understand tragedy is not, as Aristotle said, to look for the tragic flaw in the tragic hero, but the way to understand tragedy is, rather, to see that people get caught, that individuals can sometimes be caught in these movements, these conflicting forces, and the result is tragedy for them but in a way a step forward for humanity. Hegel's favorite tragedy, accordingly, is not *Oedipus* so much as *Antigone* because *Antigone* is the classic play that presents a young woman who is caught and has to make a terrible choice. On the one hand, there is the whole of what Hegel refers to as the divine law, the law of the family and family obligation. To obey that law, she has to bury her brother because Greek religion was very clear that, if you are unburied, essentially you are damned.

On the other hand, the civil leader tells her, "You cannot bury your brother; he is not to be given that kind of religious sanction," and she has a horrible choice. If she obeys the laws of the state, the laws of civil society, then she betrays her brother. If she obeys the family law and buries her brother, she betrays the state, and, of course, in the end she has to die. But the important point is that tragedy is not because Antigone has a flaw. Tragedy is because she is caught at a very critical moment in human history, the time when families and tribes are developing the larger units, what we now call societies, in which the rule is not of the father, but, rather, the rule is of law, and so tragedy gets explained by appeal to something larger than the individual, but it is not something otherworldly.

Higgins: One thing that's a bit ironic is that Hegel has a notion that we are all one, and that's part of the resolution of what seems to be a tension or a mystery about why tragedy would appeal and be so important to the Greeks, and that's something that Nietzsche refers to as well. Similarly, Schopenhauer, another person whose theory of tragedy Nietzsche is playing off here, is someone who thinks that fundamentally we are all one. Indeed, in the birth of tragedy, Nietzsche acknowledges a debt to Schopenhauer but, nevertheless, still wants to move past Schopenhauer's theory.

Schopenhauer's theory, which we will talk about in greater detail next time, is a theory that basically sees tragedy as allowing us insight into the importance of compassion, of recognizing that other people are really in the same boat. So, although a pessimist, thinking that inevitably there will be conflict, he sees tragedy as something that will bring us to moral insight. Nietzsche thinks to bring someone to moral insight is really to try to make tragedy seem in some ways less tragic, a means to an end. He wants to draw attention to the way the Greeks saw tragedy as something that has to be encountered and can't be simply explained.

Solomon: And, with Nietzsche, of course, ultimately the message is to love life despite suffering. It may be true that tragedy is unavoidable, but, nevertheless, tragedy—the very meaning of the word, as we are using it here—requires a certain kind of nobility, which means, to a certain extent, a kind of selflessness. This runs in a funny way against the rumor that Nietzsche was a defender of selfishness, but, nevertheless, as we will see, these two things actually go hand in hand in a very nice way because much of what we call selfishness, in fact, isn't selfish at all, and much of what we call selflessness isn't selfless at all.

But the basic picture that Nietzsche derives from the Greeks and the Dionysian is that we have to see ourselves not just as individuals but as part of a larger world, and Nietzsche consequently believes in something that hasn't been talked about that much in the last several hundred years, and that's fate. We are all fated, and that is going to define an awful lot of the rest of Nietzsche's philosophy.

Lecture Seven
Nietzsche and Schopenhauer on Pessimism

Scope:

Arthur Schopenhauer was and is the most outspoken defender of pessimism in philosophy. He was also Nietzsche's early mentor ("the first honest German atheist"). In this lecture, we provide arguments for and against pessimism, with an explanation of Schopenhauer's view and Nietzsche's struggle with it. Even when he most vigorously rejected pessimism, Nietzsche seems to have been caught in its web all through his career. As an antidote, he embraced "cheerfulness" and "gay" (*fröliche*) science, but it is not convincing.

Outline

I. What is pessimism? Life is more pain than pleasure. It is also meaningless.

  A. As atheists, both Schopenhauer and Nietzsche viewed the world as lacking the meaning that a providential plan would bestow.

   1. Schopenhauer compared human beings' cycle of life and death to that of insects.

   2. Life simply repeats itself endlessly without meaning, as it does for irrational animals.

   3. Humans occupy just another stage in the evolution of life; they are nothing special.

  B. Schopenhauer's pessimism turns on his idea of the Will as ultimate reality. Schopenhauer viewed all existence as one (he was the first Western philosopher to take the religion of the Far East seriously).

  C. In his book, *The World as Will and Idea*, Schopenhauer distinguished the world as representation (Immanuel Kant's "phenomenal" world), which is illusion, and the world as it really is, a dynamic but purposeless Will, which is singular but conflicted.

   1. For Kant, the world as it really is (the "noumenal" world) is the realm of God and human freedom; the phenomenal world is the everyday world.

2. Schopenhauer's "noumenal" world is chaotic, unintelligent, and driven.

3. The entire phenomenal world is just a manifestation of the Will.

D. Schopenhauer's conception of the Will is clearly one of the sources of Nietzsche's Dionysian.

1. The world as Will without purpose manifests in each of us as desire, most dramatically as sexual desire. It is thus "the will to life," and what we take to be our individual desires are in fact the desire of life itself to continue itself.

2. But what this means is that our desires cannot possibly be satisfied, that seeming satisfaction will always be followed by further desire, that our desire for a finally fulfilling life is impossible. Life ends with death and the ultimate frustration of desire.

II. There is no meaning of life in a world without purpose. Schopenhauer is an atheist, and in this he clearly differs from his mentor Kant. For Kant, God gives purpose and meaning to the world.

A. But death has no significance in a world of Will without purpose either.

1. The death of the individual is an illusion.

2. The Will itself lives on.

B. There is a respite from the Will in art and aesthetic contemplation.

1. Schopenhauer draws on Plato's ideas of the Forms, which are the prototypes for individual things (e.g., many individual things participate in the Form of Beauty).

2. Schopenhauer claimed that artists present the Forms, the universal nature of types of things, when they represent individual objects in their works.

3. When we view things aesthetically, we view them not as individual things but as instantiations of a universal form. The subject is will-less and de-individuated at such a moment. We are temporarily liberated from desire.

4. Unlike the representational arts, music is the direct manifestation of the Will and its dynamic movements.

5. It bypasses external things and touches directly on what is universal within us.
6. The arts thus allow us a respite from our desires temporarily.
7. Schopenhauer draws on the Buddhist notion of life as suffering and on the idea of transcending desire as the only means of ending suffering.

III. Nietzsche takes the aesthetic perspective to be not just an escape from suffering life but as the very meaning of life.
   A. In *Birth of Tragedy*, he tells us, "only as an aesthetic phenomenon is the world justified."
      1. Nietzsche contends that Schopenhauer's pessimism is not convincing. Nietzsche suggests "cheerfulness" and creativity, which he manifests in his own life and works.
      2. Optimism based on white-washing is also no solution.
   B. For Nietzsche, reason will not provide an answer to "the meaning of life." Rather, the meaning of life is to be found in the passions.

Essential Reading:

Birth of Tragedy in Richard Schacht, ed., *Nietzsche: Selections*.

Supplemental Reading:

Julian Young, *Nietzsche's Philosophy of Art*, Chapter 4.

Questions to Consider:

1. Is death something to be feared? Why should we fear non-being?
2. In what sense is aesthetic contemplation a relief from our struggles in the world? How does it provide this?

Lecture Seven—Transcript
Nietzsche and Schopenhauer on Pessimism

In this lecture, we would like to talk about Schopenhauer, one of Nietzsche's definitive influences. But, more generally, we would like to broach the question of pessimism, that view that the world and life really are no good. Pessimism, by one consideration, might be thought of as a kind of quantitative measure. Take the question, "Is your life more pleasure or more pain?" and, of course, most of my twenty-year-old students argue without hesitation that it is much more pleasure. I remind them that it's not over yet, and I tell them some of the things that might happen to them and some of the things that certainly will happen to them as they get older, and, of course, in the end we are all dead. They get very disturbed by this, but they are still perfectly willing to assert or at least hope that the balance will be in favor of pleasure.

Schopenhauer doesn't believe that. Schopenhauer seems to feel that life is basically suffering and that the amount of pleasure, well, take it, enjoy it, but it really isn't what life is all about. This quantitative idea that life is more pain than pleasure is, of course, subject to many different objections. For one thing, just the notion of quantification is itself rather difficult. How do we know what we are quantifying when we quantify pleasure and pain? Nietzsche would want to say, more to the point, that pleasure and pain aren't really what life is about, but there's a different kind of way of thinking about pessimism that is far more philosophical. The more philosophical way of thinking about pessimism is that life doesn't have a purpose or life doesn't have a meaning.

There are several different ways that this might be argued: one, and perhaps the most common, particularly in the nineteenth century and now the twentieth, is that what gives meaning and purpose to the world is God. Schopenhauer is an atheist. In fact, Nietzsche says, in praise of Schopenhauer, that he is the first honest German atheist. If there is no God, one might argue, then the world doesn't have a purpose, there is nothing to guide us, no ultimate goals are given to us, and the world itself has no meaning. If you look at the world as a naturalist, and, in particular, if you look at the world, as both Schopenhauer and Nietzsche tend to do, through the eyes of a biologist, then you can sort of see the point.

What Schopenhauer argues in exquisite detail, because he really knew a lot about the life sciences of his day, is that, if you look at how creatures live, there is basically just one continuous cycle to it, and to talk about it having an ultimate meaning or purpose really doesn't make much sense. He used as an example one of those many insects that develop over a long larval stage, emerge—in some cases for a single day in their full maturity—to mate, after which they quickly die, and their offspring, after spending some time in the larval stage, emerge fully grown, mate, and die. And this cycle goes on, in many cases, for millions of years. What does that add up to? It's just a cycle of life and death, but it doesn't add up to anything. It has no ultimate purpose; it has no ultimate meaning.

Watch your dog through his or her daily life, weekly life, monthly life, yearly life. We watch our dogs, whom we adore, now at age eleven, and there's a sense in which they are now slow puppies. There's a sense in which what they want out of life is pretty much what they wanted out of life when they were ten weeks old. There's a sense in which they have no anticipation of what is going to happen to them; not too soon, I hope. There's a sense in which what they do is they live for what they want to do that day. In fact, we sometimes joke that, when a dog and especially when a puppy wakes up in the morning, it's not just a brand new day, it's a brand new life. There's this sense, dogs can have a wonderful life. I often envy it, but the truth is, What does a dog's life add up to? That, I presume, is what's meant by the phrase, "a dog's life" because most dogs don't live badly at all.

Nevertheless, it doesn't add up to anything. It doesn't have a purpose; it doesn't have a meaning, and that, quite frankly, doesn't have all that much to do with whether or not dogs believe in God. The idea of life simply going on, fulfilling itself, repeating itself, is really the heart of a certain kind of pessimism. I remember a cartoon that was popular just a couple of months ago, and it was essentially one of these cartoons about evolution. In the first frame there was a little creature crawling out of the water, and, in its little bubble mind, it was thinking, "Eat, survive, reproduce." Then it had another creature that was clearly a land creature and, in its little bubble mind, said, "Eat, survive, reproduce. Eat, survive, reproduce." Then they had something that looked like a primitive primate, who was thinking, "Eat, survive, reproduce," and the final frame was a human being who was scratching his head and saying, "What's it all mean?"

It seems to characterize very well that, on the one hand, we are just another step in evolution. (Although I should point out that Schopenhauer was writing before Darwin), we are just another step in evolution. We are animals, but, nevertheless, the idea that we are somehow special, that we are in a position to discover the meaning of life, is an illusion. Now why is that? Because Schopenhauer had a view—and, in fact, it's remarkably similar to his arch rival, Hegel, who was at one point teaching in the same university, Berlin, at the same time—and that is the view that the world is one, that it's a unity, that there is really one reality underlying all things.

Schopenhauer, however, takes this view not from Hegel, whom he despised, nor does he even take it directly from the ancient Greeks, who sometimes held similar views, but, much to his credit, Schopenhauer was the first philosopher to take seriously the philosophy of the Far East, Indian philosophy in particular, and he knew Buddhism, he knew a good deal about Hinduism, and the philosophy of Brahmin that I mentioned before, the philosophy that the world is really one reality, was a philosophy that he embraced. But that one reality had a peculiar characteristic. It was in the terms that were widely used at the time. It was Will. Now the important thing for Schopenhauer is to understand what that means.

The notion of Will was used very centrally by the great German philosopher who preceded him—and he was certainly Schopenhauer's model—Immanuel Kant. For Kant, will was first of all something that each of us exercised, and Will was necessarily rational. That doesn't mean that everything we do is rational, but it means that to have a Will and to have reason and to have morality, or at least to have the understanding of morality, these are all of a package. In Schopenhauer, the will is no longer individual. The Will is, in fact, the one reality, and we know the Will through ourselves, but, nevertheless, what we know through ourselves is reality as such. But, of course, there is something else we know, too, and, to put it very simply, it's the world.

In Kant, that old picture that comes from the Greeks, Plato and Aristotle in particular—the picture that comes through the history of Christianity of two worlds: one a kind of immediate secular world and the other of a more perfect world—takes the very sophisticated variation that, on one hand, there is the world of our experience, what Kant calls the phenomenal world, and then, on the other hand, there's the world as it is in itself, that is, as the world would be if we did not perceive it through all of our senses.

Now, that's an impossible notion, and Kant realizes that's an empty notion for us. But, nevertheless, God sees the world or knows the world in a way that is very different from the way we know the world. So that notion of the world in itself is something that Kant distinguishes from the world of our experience.

What's more, that world as it is in itself has a function. It is, perhaps first and foremost, the realm of God; it is the otherworldly. It is also, however, the realm of human freedom and human action, and what we experience in ourselves, in fact, is the freedom to act, which is something different from seeing ourselves as just participants in the world. So, with this dichotomy, Schopenhauer then says the following, and this is a combination of Kant and Buddhism, "The world as phenomenon, the world of experience, is to a large extent a world of illusion. On the other hand, the world that we experience inside, the world of the Will, that's the real world, and, what's more, it's not individual Will, but all Wills are ultimately one."

Most importantly, this will is not rational. This will doesn't have an ultimate purpose, as Kant certainly thinks it does. The Will is really, I always think of it, as something like a tornado. It's something that sort of swirls around and strives inside of us and throws us from one place to the other. It's always presenting us with goals and demands, desires, but it doesn't stop; it can't be satisfied. Perhaps the most illustrative example, one that Schopenhauer actually uses quite often, that all of us can relate to, is sexual desire. Think, for example, when you were a teenager and just discovering this. The experience was that here is this enormous force speaking to you from inside of you and, at the time, you had no idea where it was coming from, where it was going, what you were supposed to do with it. What you recognized, what you could not but recognize was its power and its force. Well, you got more sophisticated. You realized there are ways of answering this desire. But are there ways of satisfying it? The answer is "no."

Goethe, in fact, says at one point, "From desire, of course, I rush to satisfaction, but, from satisfaction, I leap to desire." The truth is that satisfaction is always followed by desire. Sexual satisfaction is very brief, and the desire comes back, and this cycle continues throughout life. In fact, one can ask the following question, "What is it you desire when you have sexual desire?" Now, of course, in immediate personal terms it might just be, "I want to make love to this person that I love," or it might just be, "I want an evening's entertainment," or it might be, "I want to prove I am a man," or "I want to prove I am a beautiful woman," but all that's beside the point.

The truth is it is the Will speaking from within us, the Will as the demand for the continuation of the species, but there we are right back to where the dogs and the insects that mate one day of their lives, and lower creatures as well, are. It is simply life insisting on reproducing itself, the species insisting on going on, but, if the question is, Why? There is no answer to that. We are simply buffered by the Will, and that's the end of it.

Higgins: Now, that's a pretty bleak picture. The story of the universe that Schopenhauer tells doesn't give us much consolation. The one perhaps potentially consoling thing is that Schopenhauer claims that, along with our general sense of satisfying our individual desires— something he claims is an illusion—he also thinks that it is really an illusion to concern ourselves with our individual existence. Ultimately we are all one thing, and although, for many of us, an overwhelming preoccupation is a concern with the fact that we are mortal, Schopenhauer claims that this is really a kind of illusory problem. If we are all this fundamental one force that expresses itself in nature, our individual death really doesn't mean much of anything.

In effect, what goes on, nature, is really all that we were originally. So we might take comfort in the thought that what's really real in us, what's important in us, continues despite our individual demise. Nevertheless, not too many people find that all that reassuring, and Schopenhauer is well aware of it. The generally pessimistic tone of his writing has a lot to do with the fact that he thinks most of us aren't going to take any solace in that and are not going to draw the appropriate conclusions. He does, however, mention a couple of ways that many of us at least avoid dwelling on what's unpleasant for us. He thinks that there is a kind of respite from willing and either getting satisfied and briefly bored or willing, getting satisfied, and immediately willing again.

The main way in which people take a kind of break from all this is through aesthetic experience. Indeed, I think it is noteworthy that, whereas Schopenhauer paints a very pessimistic and disturbing picture of the world as a whole, his specific examples indicate, just in the way he writes about them, a kind of aesthetic appreciation. He takes joy in learning about biological examples and, even though the upshot is often exactly what Bob described, a kind of sense that this is a continuing saga that ultimately signifies nothing, nevertheless, one gets the impression that he really takes great delight in observing and recognizing the ways in which nature works. Schopenhauer's own theory acknowledges that this is the main way that a lot of us find at least temporary meaning in our lives. He talks about aesthetic experience as a kind of sabbath from the penal servitude of willing.

His conception of aesthetic experiences draws on yet another of his philosophical heroes besides the Buddha and Kant, namely, Plato. He draws from Plato's notion of the forms or ideas prototypes for the particular individual things that we observe in the phenomenal world. According to Plato, for example, when we see something beautiful, we are seeing an instance that has many, many different illustrations, an instance of something that participates in a fundamental pattern, absolute beauty, and, in a sense, when we recognize beauty in the here and now in a particular thing, we are actually turning our minds towards something that is more fundamental, universal, and eternal, namely, beauty itself.

Schopenhauer's way of dealing with this notion of forms is to say that most artists depict particular things but in a way that makes us mindful of these universal prototypes or patterns. So a sculptor that, for instance, sculpts a wolf will, in a sense, have in mind the basic prototype or pattern of a wolf, and it will be the universal notion of wolfness, you might say, that comes through in what the artist does to the extent the artist really is in control of his or her art. What this does for us in terms of willing is it allows us an occasion to simply rest content with contemplating. Once again the kind of contemplation we discussed in an earlier lecture becomes a very significant and important component of life.

As Schopenhauer sees it, when we can just contemplate the basic patterns of the world, we no longer have our usual disposition, which is to gaze around us and itemize things in terms of things that I want, things I don't want, things that help me get what I want, or things that obstruct me. All of those kinds of relations we have to things tend to put us in a rather aggressive, antagonistic, and ultimately frustrated state of mind toward the rest of reality. When we observe something in an aesthetic light, however—and Schopenhauer here would include beautiful nature along with art—what we do is transport our gaze away from particular objects of desire for me, the individual, to the universal beauty of this type of thing.

Similarly, when I do that, I am no longer relating to myself as an individual that either does or does not get what I desire. Instead, I think of myself as a kind of universal being as well. If I gaze at the universal form of something through a particular in art or beautiful nature, at the same time I am making myself a kind of universal case of a human being contemplating. Schopenhauer calls this the pure willess subject of knowledge. I am willess because I am not relating to myself as a private person with desires, perhaps with greed, but instead thinking of myself as the mind, the mind of the human being. And, with that, I at least take a break from willing, trying to get what I want. For the time being, I don't even think about desire.

Unfortunately, this blessed state of mind doesn't last very long. For the most part, we go to an art gallery and perhaps experience beauty but eventually get hungry and turn our minds back to desire. If we're particularly unfortunate, we might even start thinking about desiring art itself, wanting to own rather than simply contemplate. So Schopenhauer thinks sooner or later, inevitably, desire catches up with us again. There is, however, one other aesthetic kind of appreciation that he discusses and that Nietzsche draws upon, actually, the aesthetic appreciation we have of music. Now, Schopenhauer, being a nineteenth-century thinker, does not have in mind the kind of abstract visual arts that are very common fare today. He tends to think of all the visual arts as presenting depictions or representations.

On the other hand, he thinks of music as something that is much more formal. Music doesn't seem to be mimicking anything in particular in the world, although we feel that it has a very intimate connection with our world, and Schopenhauer's way of understanding this, again a theme that Nietzsche picks up on, is that, in music, what we have is something like a representation of the Will itself, the way in which the Will moves through nature, the kind of inner conflict of the Will, which we might see in musical dissonance and its resolution in stages of relative consonants, for example. Schopenhauer is convinced that the reason we find music so moving is it bypasses representing things in the external world and we feel more that it is intimately in connection with this inner stirring, the Will as it acts in ourselves.

So a musical condition is particularly important for us because, again, it draws our attention to what's universal within us, the very phenomena of the Will manifesting itself through us, and, by doing that, it makes us again mindful of our real existence, ourselves as members of a species, manifestations of a Will that fundamentally makes us all one. However, like the visual arts, music usually doesn't sustain us through a lifetime. Even though we might be transported by the occasional concert, most likely we spend much of our life willing, getting frustrated, willing, getting satisfied and bored, and then willing again. The only ultimate solution for human beings is really to somehow move one's sense of self away from personal, private aims—the kind of everyday willing that we all engage in—to shift from that sense of who we are to a totally universalized concept, and that, he thinks, is something that the saints of various traditions have achieved.

Schopenhauer's conception of life being full of frustration and desire draws a lot from the Buddhist notion of life being suffering, and Schopenhauer also follows the Buddha in suggesting that the only real solution to this is to get over this kind of continual craving. So, if we can manage to start to see ourselves as really the same self as everyone else, competing with them for particular good things that we want seems rather pointless. If we really register this, if we really come to take this to heart, then the whole project of willing, trying to get what we individually desire, starts to seem more and more pointless. And, if we really do maintain this kind of insight, then what will happen naturally is we will simply stop. We will come to a state of what Schopenhauer describes as resignation. We will resign from willing.

Now how does all this relate to Nietzsche? Nietzsche tends to follow Schopenhauer a long way in this account. Nietzsche, as we discussed in earlier lectures, was quite convinced that life does entail a certain amount of frustration, downright suffering, and ultimate death. So he thinks Schopenhauer is certainly pursuing the right track to try to encourage us to think about this, to recognize the truth of this and not whitewash it. On the other hand, Nietzsche thinks that Schopenhauer perhaps gives aesthetic experience a little bit too short shrift. As Nietzsche sees it, there is a kind of aesthetic way of dealing with the whole problem of individual frustration, suffering, and death. He comments, in *The Birth of Tragedy*, "only as an aesthetic phenomenon is this life eternally justified."

In other words, Nietzsche is suggesting that there is a kind of answer to the problem of evil that aesthetics—art—can provide, and this particular answer is an answer that has to do with seeing the world, in a sense, from this point of view of ourselves as universal. Instead of thinking of ourselves as just one more phenomenon fighting it out with the rest, as we observe the world as an aesthetic phenomenon, we think of the way all of these things go together. Nietzsche thinks if we really do this it doesn't really matter to us as much that we are in the competition, in the general fray, and sometimes get frustrated during the course of it. That's simply what participating in life involves or entails, and that, he thinks, is something that we can come to grips with and actually appreciate so long as we maintain awareness that that's our individual participation in this much bigger thing, this, in a sense, more real thing: life as a whole.

One might compare the way that Schopenhauer and Nietzsche think differently on these issues by noting that Schopenhauer really thinks that ultimate satisfaction is what we really want and that we are going to be frustrated unless we get to a state where we are completely content. Nietzsche thinks that that really doesn't have much to do with life as it is lived, and, if we think about it, isn't really what we want. The nature of life is to be in a state of continual change, a state of movement, a state, if you want to call it this, of frustration, but that this frustration is actually something we can appreciate itself, something along the lines of our appreciation of musical dissonance, which is a state, a particular moment in music, where you certainly have the sense that you need to move from that, but that moving itself is what life consists of.

Strangely, although Schopenhauer shares many of the presuppositions that Nietzsche does, Nietzsche thinks Schopenhauer is really looking for a kind of stasis, a state of perfect contentment where you don't need to strive anymore. You're finally fully satisfied, and Nietzsche thinks what we ought to throw out is not our desires but the sense that a kind of position of perfect satisfaction is either attainable or desirable. So Nietzsche does, in a sense, take a more optimistic view than Schopenhauer. He buys the pessimistic premise that starts Schopenhauer's own philosophy, the premise that, indeed, individuals are inevitably subject to suffering and death.

But, nevertheless, he thinks that we need not look at this as a kind of argument against the value of life. Taking a kind of source of sustenance from being part of life, from being part of the motion, or the dynamic of life rather than looking for a peaceful state in which to live out your days is what we ought to do. Despite this relative optimism, however, Nietzsche is not favoring a kind of cheap whitewashing of reality. He tends to think that too much focus on optimism—as in some people who look at the Greeks and say, "Oh, how cheerful they were"—he thinks that's not really a good thing, either, that we should recognize that life involves these various negative components but, nevertheless, that we should approach the world with what he calls strong pessimism, a sense that we can really deal with this and even take joy in it.

Solomon: Nietzsche's role of optimism, or what he often calls cheerfulness, I find not always convincing. You get the sense that here is a man who desperately wants to feel good about life and cheerful, but, nevertheless, there's a sense that, throughout his entire life, he is really saddled with Schopenhauer's pessimism or a version of it and is trying to convince himself that life is really worthwhile despite all of the suffering. But this leads to another way of looking at pessimism and looking at the meaning of life. Schopenhauer ultimately seems to think that meaning, purpose, is to be found in a kind of rationality. That's what Kant thought.

Nevertheless, what Nietzsche points out, and I think very powerfully, is that the meaning of life is to be found not in reason, not in rationality, not in some calculation, much less in theology, but the meaning of life is to be found in the passions, that it's creativity, it's being devoted to causes, it's being dedicated to something—another person, a project, an art. That's what gives life meaning, and so pessimism is overcome as the aesthetic phenomenon, not as a reason, not as a rational enterprise, but, rather, by something you really care about, something you feel deeply passionate about.

Lecture Eight
Nietzsche, Jesus, Zarathustra

Scope:

Nietzsche was a scholar not only of ancient Greece (and Rome) but also a scholar and both fan and harsh critic of the Old Testament Prophets and Jesus and the Gospels. He was also well read on the history and teachings of the Persian sage Zarathustra (Latin name, Zoroaster). Nietzsche's best known book is *Thus Spoke Zarathustra*, a Biblical parody in which the Persian prophet is depicted as rejecting all "otherworldly" ways of living, notably Christianity. It is in *Zarathustra* that Nietzsche introduces the idea of the *Übermensch*. He also introduces the idea of "the last man," the perfectly happy "couch potato."

Outline

I. Nietzsche follows the Old Testament prophets in his attempt to understand the failings of his era ("modernity") and anticipate the consequences to come.

II. Nietzsche may attack Christianity but he retains his admiration for Jesus. He also attacked Socrates but nevertheless obviously admires him (for example, in connection with Socrates' emphasis on rule by wise individuals).

    A. Nietzsche saw in Jesus a prophet who accurately diagnosed many of the weaknesses of both the Roman and the Jewish ways of life but was misunderstood.

    B. He also came to see Socrates as a prophet of sorts who tried to radically change society in some directions that Nietzsche found quite congenial.

    C. Nietzsche's view of both Jesus and Socrates is a mixture of disapproval, admiration, and envy. He does not, as did Hegel, starkly contrast them.

    D. Nietzsche appreciated the Gospels, as he appreciated Plato, as the true creators of the Jesus and Socrates legends, respectively.

III. Nietzsche used the Persian prophet Zarathustra to create a similar legend, but to very different ends.

A. Zarathustra, unlike Jesus and Socrates, preached *against* the otherworldly in favor of "love of the earth."

    1. Zarathustra is a counterpart to Jesus and Socrates.

    2. In the opening of Nietzsche's work, Zarathustra is compared to the philosopher in Plato's "Myth of the Cave" and to Jesus as he prepares for his mission.

B. Nietzsche drew from what is known about the historical Zarathustra.

    1. Zarathustra lived during a changing political situation.

    2. He offered a new way to interpret the success that invading nomads had against the Persians' established agrarian settlements.

    3. Zarathustra discouraged worship of the traditional deities who were also worshipped by the Persians' enemies to the East. Although acknowledging the existence of other deities, he called for worship of a Supreme God, Ahura Mazda.

    4. Zarathustra is therefore described as the founder of Western monotheism.

C. *Thus Spoke Zarathustra* is an epic poem in quasi-Biblical style in which the central character, Zarathustra, repeatedly emerges from his mountain solitude to meet and persuade the odd caricatures of humanity of his doctrines.

    1. Nietzsche's Zarathustra is based on the real historical figure, but one of the central theses, the rejection of the distinction between good and evil, is the opposite of one of Zarathustra's most famous teachings.

    2. Zarathustra emphasized the need for distinguishing between good and evil. But Nietzsche does not think Zarathustra would stop with this simplistic dichotomy, as did the subsequent moral tradition.

    3. Zarathustra made his distinction in response to the situation of his time. In our time, he would be proposing new ideas for living meaningfully without the dead myth of the Christian God.

    4. Nietzsche was thus continuing the original Zarathustra's work; Zarathustra has evolved into Nietzsche.

D. Nietzsche next introduces the "Three Metamorphoses," from camel to lion to child.

    1. The camel takes on the burdens of the tradition.

    2. The lion declares his superiority to the received tradition.

    3. The child approaches the world with a keen sense of play and inventiveness; this is a vision of a new innocence.

E. Nietzsche also introduces the *Übermensch*. The *Übermensch* appears only in *Thus Spoke Zarathustra*.

    1. The *Übermensch* is not an evolutionary goal.

    2. The *Übermensch* is more comparable to the image of the child in "The Three Metamorphoses." The *Übermensch* represents vitality and risk-taking.

F. Nietzsche also introduces "the last man," an image of where we may actually be headed as a species.

    1. The last man has no ambition, takes no risks, represents the end of the continual cycle of regeneration.

    2. Zarathustra's own efforts indicate his opposition to the last man's selfish obsession with comfort.

IV. In the opening of the book's Prologue, Zarathustra says he will "go under." This is a play on the German word "*untergehen*," which is used for both the setting of the sun (which cyclically recurs) and for dying.

A. Zarathustra is willing to throw himself and his life fully into his work, his mission to humanity, despite its risks. He recognizes that he will eventually perish in the process.

B. Zarathustra's efforts are more often frustrated than successful, perhaps a confession and an anticipation on Nietzsche's part of his own influence.

C. Zarathustra often fails to make himself understood (e.g., his hearers misunderstand his reference to "the last man") and he often feels himself to be a failure.

Recommended Reading:

Thus Spoke Zarathustra, in Richard Schacht, ed. *Nietzsche: Selections*.

Supplemental Reading:

Kathleen M. Higgins, *Nietzsche's* Zarathustra.

————, "Reading *Zarathustra*," in Robert C. Solomon, Kathleen M. Higgins, eds., *Reading Nietzsche*, pp. 132–151.

Questions to Consider:

1. Could we view Nietzsche as a prophet? What is his prophecy?

2. How do you envision Nietzsche's *Übermensch*? What does it represent?

Lecture Eight—Transcript
Nietzsche, Jesus, Zarathustra

In this lecture I am going to talk about one of Nietzsche's works that, in a sense, is an aberration from the way he often writes. This is actually the book that he thinks is his most important or claims to at times—*Thus Spoke Zarathustra*. Most of Nietzsche's works, as we've discussed, are either in essay form or, very commonly, aphoristic form. But *Thus Spoke Zarathustra* is the only work in which he makes a sort of sustained stab at fiction, although a highly philosophical kind of fiction. So what I am going to be discussing are perhaps some of his bases for choosing this form in the first place and some of the very interesting ideas that come out in the book.

One way of getting a sense of why Nietzsche might have chosen to write about a Persian prophet, and one that wasn't all that well-known in Europe, was that Nietzsche saw in Zarathustra a kind of counterpart to some of the heroes, indeed, his own heroes, from his own tradition. Nietzsche has in mind his heroes—despite the kind of obvious sense in which they aren't heroes—Jesus and Socrates, as having been the beginners of a tradition that he thought basically went downhill. Strangely enough, although Jesus and Socrates would seem to be representatives of exactly what Nietzsche disliked about this tradition, he seems to think that, for all of what he sees as false in their tradition, these men were some of the most important people in world history and also, in a certain sense, his philosophical rivals.

For example, he tends to think of both of them as something like the Hebrew prophets, people who were critical of the excesses of their times and people who had ideas about how to reform the world in what they thought was a better way. Nietzsche himself certainly thinks that that typical kind of project is something he wants to do for his own time. So, in that, he thought that Jesus and Socrates were both, in a sense, similar or kindred spirits. Also, more specifically, there were ideas that Jesus and Socrates had that he tended to think well of. For example, in Socrates' case, Socrates suggested the idea of the philosopher king, that the rule by a king should not be something that is a matter simply of party politics, but, instead, people should choose leaders on the basis of their wisdom, and institutions should be arranged in that kind of way. These are ideas that Nietzsche is quite sympathetic to.

Similarly, in the case of Jesus, Jesus himself was a great critic of people in his own religious tradition as well as some of the excesses of behavior in the Roman Empire, and Nietzsche similarly felt that that was a very reasonable kind of approach to their life and times. Interestingly, though, in the case of both Jesus and Socrates, the way that history has come to know these figures is not through their own writings, but through the writings of others. In the case of Jesus, this is the Four Evangelists, and, in the case of Socrates, it's Plato's dialogues. In a sense, what Nietzsche is trying to do in *Zarathustra* is to write something comparable to the New Testament or to the Platonic dialogues and to focus on a different hero, but a hero in a sense of the same kind of stature as Jesus and Socrates, namely, in a sense, the West's earliest philosopher, Zarathustra.

Zarathustra, as many of you may know, was a famous Persian prophet, indeed, the first religious hero that we tend to hear about in that part of the Middle East. What Nietzsche found interesting about Zarathustra, I think, was that Zarathustra, in a sense, was one of the earliest religious spokespeople, the founder of a new religion and a new religion that tended to have its consequence for later religious traditions in the West. To say a bit about the historical Zarathustra, he lived in a time when things were starting to change in his own location. India and Persia had both largely been part of the same religious tradition up until this point, and the political situation had started to change when some people settled down in stable communities whereas other people remained nomadic, as had been the general practice in the region. Zarathustra's appearance on the scene came at a time when there was a lot of concern about the fact that those who had settled were constantly being victimized by raiders who would come in on horseback and take food, take whatever they wanted to, basically, and, not surprisingly in a case where there was a lot of pain going on, there was a tendency to think of this in terms of religion.

So, for instance, many of Zarathustra's contemporaries tended to think that, if these invaders were actually succeeding in taking things from their community, their gods must be stronger. What Zarathustra did was, in a sense, to separate the Persian religion from the Indian tradition of which it had been a part. Zarathustra insisted that some of the deities that had been worshipped in the past, namely, the divas—the very deities that we tend to learn about in the Hindu pantheon to this day—should not be worshipped. If people in the settled communities of Persia were worshipping them, in a sense they were adding to their power, and this power seemed to be what was actually allowing their enemies to come in and take things out of their city. So, instead, what they should do is stop all of that worship and instead focus on the worship of a different kind of deity, the Ahura, and particularly a Supreme Ahura, Ahura Mazda, the Supreme God.

In this sense, Zarathustra was the founder of Western monotheism. It is a qualified monotheism, to be sure; the idea of worshipping a supreme God didn't equate in Zarathustra's mind to the idea that there was only one god. There were other gods, other deities, it's just that they weren't as powerful and shouldn't be encouraged, in some cases. Nevertheless, there was a kind of move in the direction that later Judaism, Christianity, and Islam all followed—the idea of a single God to whom worship should be focused. More interestingly, in a way, from Nietzsche's point of view, Zarathustra's main religious innovation besides this claim that this single supreme God should be the focus of worship was the idea that good and evil should be distinguished.

This is particularly interesting in Nietzsche's case because Nietzsche actually takes issue with the way good and evil have been understood in his own tradition. So the fact that he's chosen, as his spokesperson, in a way, a person who founded the idea of taking this as a very serious dichotomy, is something that in a way needs to be explained. Strangely enough, I think, the tendency oftentimes in reading Nietzsche's book *Zarathustra* is not to notice that he is placing so much emphasis on the original simply because his Zarathustra talks about modern problems and so on. Nevertheless, it is very clear Nietzsche did have the historical Zarathustra in part in mind when he wrote the opening. The way he concluded the book that he had finished right before *Zarathustra* was to present a kind of arrival of Zarathustra on the scene, and he basically takes this same section as the opening for *Thus Spoke Zarathustra*. So I will read this passage in full and then comment:

"When Zarathustra was thirty years old, he left his home and Lake Urmi and went into the mountains. There he enjoyed his spirit and his solitude and for ten years did not tire of that, but at last his heart changed and one morning he rose with the dawn, stepped before the sun, and spoke to it thus, 'You great star, what would your happiness be if you did not have those for whom you shine? For ten years you have climbed up to my cave. You would have become weary of your light and of the journey had it not been for me and my eagle and my serpent, but we waited for you every morning, took your overflow from you, and blessed you for it. Behold, I am sick of my wisdom. Like a bee that has gathered too much honey, I need hands outstretched to receive it.

'I want to give away and distribute until the wise among men enjoy their folly once again and the poor their riches. For that I must descend to the depths as you do in the evening when you go behind the sea and still bring light to the underworld, you over-rich star. Like you, I must go under, as men put it to whom I wish to descend. Bless me then, your calm eye that can look without envy even upon an all too great happiness. Bless the cup that wants to overflow in order that the water may flow from it golden and carry the reflection of your rapture everywhere. Behold, this cup wants to become empty again, and Zarathustra wants to become man again.' Thus Zarathustra began to go under."

Now, a number of features of that opening, I think, are extremely interesting, one of which is that it's quasi-biblical in style. We have an invocation, a kind of hymn to a god, in effect, as Zarathustra begins this journey. And though Zarathustra, in Nietzsche's story, is going to be, in a sense, a spokesperson for his atheistic view of the world, nevertheless, there is this opening in which Zarathustra certainly is positioned as a kind of religious prophet. I think that is a clear indication that Nietzsche has a historical Zarathustra in mind. He also mentions explicitly Lake Urmi, which is the vicinity of the area that the original Zarathustra lived in, and apparently the story goes that Zarathustra did live in a mountain cave.

Another thing that comes true in this kind of quasi-biblical invocation is the way in which Zarathustra is being presented as a kind of counterpart to Jesus and also to Socrates: to Jesus in the sense that he begins his mission at the age of thirty, or at least we hear mention of him at the age of thirty, in a sense stopping and reflecting—going into retirement—before beginning a mission to humanity. Immediately Zarathustra is unlike Christ, who went briefly into the desert forty days, was tempted there, and immediately launched into his mission to humanity. Zarathustra, by contrast, stayed in solitude for ten years and only descends to

©1999 The Teaching Company.

humanity later on. But when he does descend to humanity, there is a kind of reference to a very famous story in the Platonic dialogues.

Plato's *Republic* includes Socrates' story, "The Myth of the Cave," in which he speaks of people who have spent their whole lives chained in a cave and who basically see only shadows cast against the wall by things moving around between a fire in back of them and the screen, in effect, of a wall, and, therefore, their whole world, their whole sense of what's out there, is just these shadows. The story goes that one of them was able to escape the cave, to go out into the world to see the sun, to see all the kinds of things in the world and suddenly sees what the real situation is. This person, according to Socrates, would be overwhelmingly full of desire to go down to his fellows in the cave and tell them what he discovered. Unfortunately, people who lived in the cave would not believe this. They knew their world, and this was not it. In addition, by changing from the very bright light of the external world to the cave again, the person returning to the cave actually seems to have lost his eyesight and therefore can be dismissed as well.

In a sense, then, Zarathustra is taking on that position of the philosopher who is returning to humanity, though, strangely enough, it was the cave in which he gained his wisdom, not spending time out in the open world of the valley. So there is a kind of attempt to turn some details of the traditional stories on their heads, and, indeed, that's what Zarathustra does. He, in a sense, is addressing the same kinds of important religious questions that he thought that Socrates and Jesus both did but at the same time in somewhat novel ways, and that's one of the structural features that I think is quite important about the book. There are all kinds of illusions to Plato and the New Testament, which indicates that Nietzsche is concerned that Zarathustra address some of the same issues but sometimes in ways that deviate considerably.

One of the very important features of the historical Zarathustra that I think is relevant here is that the historical Zarathustra was not so interested in another world. There seems to have been a kind of political motivation in the first place for his talking about gods, talking about good and evil, allying yourself with the right force and maintaining a kind of stance of firm enmity against the other. All of this had a certain kind of earthly basis, namely, the situation of his community in his time. Zarathustra is also quite adamant that people who worshiped Ahura Mazda should be agrarian. They should help to raise cattle, particularly, and also to farm, and this was part of their obligation as people that were members of the religion.

So again there is a kind of emphasis on this world as opposed to focusing all attention to another world, and, that, I think, Nietzsche would be extremely pleased about. In fact, one of the first things he has Zarathustra do as soon as he descends from the mountain is arrive in a community and claim, "I teach you the meaning of the earth." It's the meaning of the earth that's going to be important to Nietzsche's Zarathustra, not so much seeking the meaning of the earth in something completely other. Zarathustra begins his general mission after a kind of speech about teaching the meaning of the earth with a story that is a parable, a parable that isn't really located anywhere in time and place. In this respect, it resembles Hegel's famous master and slave dialectic where we have a master and slave interact, but we don't know where they are in time and space, presumably because this is a kind of model that fits lots of situations.

The story Zarathustra tells is not so much about the interaction of two different individuals but more the interaction of one individual with the whole tradition, and he tells of three stages that such an individual faces, at least if this individual evolves ideally. First of all, a spiritual person is going to adopt the stage of what Zarathustra calls the camel, the camel who would bear much, and what he has in mind here is someone who takes on the burden of the tradition, learns it thoroughly, is willing to carry it, who spends a livelihood, in a sense, carrying on things that have been learned from the tradition.

As Nietzsche sees it, this is certainly the starting point for any kind of spiritual development, and I think this is a quite interesting contrast with the way Nietzsche is often perceived. Nietzsche has often been viewed as someone who basically turned aside his tradition and wanted to do something completely different. I think this story suggests otherwise, that, indeed, the move that Nietzsche made in saying no to certain things about his tradition are already based on having absorbed the tradition and treated it with a great deal of reverence. It is only at stage two that one starts to question some of it, and this is the stage that Zarathustra describes as the lion stage.

In the stage of the lion, the soul stops simply following what the tradition has suggested and starts to evaluate and to say no, to assert individuality by questioning, challenging some of the things that have simply been handed on as the truth, and it is in this stage that perhaps we see the image of Nietzsche fitting most precisely, the idea that, having learned the tradition, suddenly a certain maturity is reached at which point questions can be asked. So no longer simply serving the tradition but saying no to parts of it becomes the important thing. However, this is not the final stage, and again this counters the common image of Nietzsche. The final stage moves beyond this "no"-saying stage where the soul is simply rejecting to a new kind of affirmation, and this final stage is characterized metaphorically as a stage of the child. The child at this point has a kind of boundless energy for what's new, for experimentation.

In one of Nietzsche's other works, he talks about how a man's maturity is returning to the kind of seriousness had at play by children, and, if you think about children at play, there is a kind of seriousness in all the games involved, but none of them are viewed as the fundamental matter of things. You finish a game and start another one. There is a kind of willingness to, in a sense, regenerate one's activities, not to be caught either in simply obeying or simply defying but having a kind of new creative energy that comes out of oneself. So the image of a child for Nietzsche is an image of full creative response and full vitality that one sees in children at play discovering the world for the first time. It's a kind of image of a new innocence.

So despite the fact that already this kind of evolution of the soul has involved learning the whole tradition, rejecting some of it, only now are you in a stage to really become a child, to start over and deal with the world in your own way, and that's what Zarathustra holds up as an ideal. Another way of capturing the notion of the ideal for Zarathustra is this famous expression "the Übermensch," the overman or superman, and, indeed, this term does come up very early in the book. In Zarathustra's first speech, after all, to his humanity that he finds gathered before him, he starts talking about teaching the overman, the overman or Übermensch being the meaning of the earth.

As we have mentioned in earlier lectures, it is not so much that Nietzsche's talking about an evolutionary goal of a straightforward sort, but I think that perhaps the best way of making some sense of the image is to think of it in terms of this image of the child. The Übermensch is someone who is like humanity in a lot of ways but more capable, having transcended a lot of human limitations. In a sense, this kind of boundless vitality of the child is something that is being presented here as a kind of ideal, a way of approaching reality, and the Übermensch as Zarathustra characterizes it is a way of being that involves risk taking, not concerning yourself so much with simply going about your everyday routine but always thinking of new ways of approaching things and not being unwilling to take risks in order to bring something better about.

The idea of having certain kinds of aspirations and being willing to stake your life on them, in a sense, is what Zarathustra thinks is really urgent, the whole idea of passion and passionate involvement. Even if you end up risking life and limb, you're spending your energy, which is finite, and your life span, which is finite, on some particular quests. Nevertheless, he thinks that's a kind of nobility that we ought to view as ideal. We ought to become heroes but not heroes of a tradition that we haven't had a part in; instead, heroes of new ways of thinking things through, of new ideas that we have developed ourselves after having being nurtured by the tradition.

The Übermensch is presented as this kind of image of an ideal way to be, and I think maybe one could consider it also a kind of general placeholder for one's notion of greatness. Exactly what it amounts to, to be great or to do something great, is going to depend very much on who you are, what time you're living in, what your circumstances are, and so on. But the idea of the Übermensch is we can always do something better. We shouldn't just view humanity and the arrival of humanity on the scene as the be-all and end-all of nature. Let us see if we can transcend the human, all too human. Maybe people have tended to have these weaknesses, but let's see if we can move beyond that.

In his opening speech, Zarathustra contrasts the Übermensch with another image, which he fears might be the actual outcome of further evolution or actually devolution, namely, what he calls the last man. The last man is a kind of caricature of really the opposite of the Übermensch, someone who will take no risks whatsoever, someone who has no ambitions whatsoever, in effect, the ultimate "couch potato" who really basically wants to be comfortable. In a way, this image is a kind of lampoon against the utilitarians who talk about trying to bring about a state where pain is minimized. Nietzsche frequently suggests that you can minimize pain by making yourself

©1999 The Teaching Company.

completely numb and avoiding any situation in which you exert yourself. But what kind of a life is that, and indeed that's how he presents the last man.

The last man is very much convinced that this way of being is great because it is calm and comforting. There is a sense in which the last man has, as Zarathustra puts it, invented happiness, but it is a very feeble kind of happiness and a happiness that doesn't see beyond the present moment. This kind of not seeing beyond the present moment makes the last man the last man. The last man, in a sense, would be the end of the road, the end of this kind of continual cycle of regeneration of which earth and human life participate. So, by comparison with Schopenhauer's story of the insect that over and over again tries to find a mate, mates, and then immediately dies only to start the cycle up again—that's a much more meaningful way of existing than the last man, who basically doesn't even have the desire to move beyond the couch.

The Übermensch, by contrast, is, in a sense, the descendant of us if we really decide to take ourselves seriously enough to make goals for ourselves, to attempt things, to attempt things that might cause us to perish in the process. An interesting aspect of the little passage I read you where Zarathustra appears is that Zarathustra is said to have decided to go under, and this is actually a play on words in German. *Untergehen*, meaning *go under*, is, on the one hand, a word that's used to describe the sun setting at the end of the day, with the idea that, although setting happens, so does regeneration when the morning comes.

Also, *untergehen* has a notion of dying or perishing. So there is a sense in which what Zarathustra decides to do is to commit himself fully to the task of extending his wisdom to others even if it kills him in the process, and any kind of work one chooses to do, in a sense, does use up your life. There is a sense in which whatever you undertake is, in a way, a route to death, and Zarathustra sees that, too. But he has made a decision at this point that what he is going to commit himself to, the work he is going to undertake in his life, is going to be this effort to return to humanity and to go under, literally, to perish in the process. Nietzsche through Zarathustra suggests that that's, in a sense, the only way to be, to decide on a project that of course you know is finite, in the sense that your life span is finite, but, nevertheless, to make something of it, to make something that you can visualize is great and to keep trying even if it isn't a completely successful experiment.

Interestingly enough, Zarathustra's own efforts aren't entirely successful. When he makes this speech, for example, he finds that a crowd has gathered for a circus, and when he is talking about the last man, they think, well, this is probably a performer. "Bring the performer out," they tell him. Zarathustra's been mistaken, in effect, for a circus barker, and there are lots of really perverse things that happen through the story—I mean, in a sense, a novel—in which Zarathustra is completely misunderstood. Much of the dynamic, I would say, of the novel has to do with failures to make him understood on Zarathustra's part and efforts he comes up with in order to overcome that. So he wants to present a story in which even presenting an individual's work, the work of Zarathustra, even though he is presenting this as kind of ideal in that he's really committed himself, it's not a completely risk-free proposition.

It has all kinds of risks involved in it, and Zarathustra often feels like a complete failure, and it is this kind of regenerating commitment to his task that tells the story of much of the novel. In this respect, I think he is drawing on what actually is another reason that Nietzsche chooses Zarathustra as a kind of spokesperson. Nietzsche himself, in talking about Zarathustra later on in his autobiography, points out that people haven't found his choice of Zarathustra nearly as interesting as he thinks it is, and he comments, "I have not been asked as I should have been asked what the name of Zarathustra means in my mouth, the mouth of the first immoralist. For what constitutes a tremendous historical uniqueness of that Persian is just the opposite of this. Zarathustra was the first to consider the fight of good and evil, the very wheel and the machinery of things. The transposition of morality into the metaphysical realm as a force, cause, an end in itself, is his work. But this question itself is at bottom its own answer.

"Zarathustra created this most calamitous error, morality; consequently, he must also be the first to recognize it. Not only has he had more experience in this matter for a longer time than any other thinker—after all, the whole of history is a refutation by experiment of the principle of the so-called moral world order—what is more important is that Zarathustra is more truthful than any other thinker. His doctrine and his alone posits truthfulness as the highest

©1999 The Teaching Company.

virtue. This means the opposite of the cowardice of the idealist who flees from reality. Zarathustra has more intestinal fortitude than all other thinkers taken together. To speak the truth and to shoot well with arrows, that is Persian virtue. Am I understood? The self-overcoming of morality out of truthfulness, the self-overcoming of the moralist into his opposite, into me, that is what the name Zarathustra means in my mouth."

I think this is really a shocking statement because he is, in effect, saying that Zarathustra, even by distinguishing good and evil, was already starting the path that led forward to Nietzsche, who puts good and evil aside, and what he is suggesting here is that what Zarathustra really did was create a kind of basic distinction where distinctions weren't being made, and, rather than follow through by making more refined distinctions, the tradition just stuck with that first one. So it treats good and evil as two, in a sense, tales into which you can place every human action. It is good or evil. Nothing more subtle need be done. And Nietzsche's view is Zarathustra, being a very truthful person, would never have seen this as the best outcome for what he attempted. What he attempted was to become more refined in one's understanding.

Similarly, the fact that Zarathustra is committed to truthfulness allies Nietzsche's Zarathustra and allies Nietzsche himself with his project, because what, in effect, happens here is that it's truthfulness, Nietzsche would claim, that has led him to question the existence of the Christian God or to question good and evil, and this is precisely, too, what his *Zarathustra* attempts to show. Zarathustra attempts to preach this kind of new vision of reality without the Christian God, and, indeed, much of the story involves his attempt to learn how to live in a meaningful way without the Christian God. He, too, sees a kind of sadness in the wake of what he views as God's death, but, with this sadness, he attempts instead to bring about a kind of way in which meaning can be understood. In that way, he thinks that he actually is continuing the work of Zarathustra, that Zarathustra has evolved into him.

Thank you.

Lecture Nine
Nietzsche on Reason, Instinct, and Passion

Scope:

Against the grain of philosophy since the Greeks, Nietzsche rejects the primacy of reason in human life. Shifting instead to biology, he defends a powerful notion of instinct and emphasizes the importance of unconscious drives in human behavior. From his early *Birth of Tragedy* to his late work *Twilight of the Idols*, Nietzsche debunks the celebration of reason and consciousness. He accuses Socrates of turning reason into a tyrant. Accordingly, Nietzsche might well be considered a "romantic" in his celebration of passion (although Nietzsche rejected romanticism as being "shallow"). We will argue that Nietzsche had great insight into the nature of emotion.

Outline

I. The primacy of reason dominates Western philosophy. The passions are typically demeaned (e.g., by Socrates, medieval philosophy, Enlightenment thought, and modern philosophy).

    A. Rationality has no clear, singular meaning.

        1. It refers, for example, to the fact that we can think, reflect and use language.

        2. It refers to the fact that we can do mathematics, "do sums" (in the words of Bertrand Russell)—emphasized by the ancient Greeks.

        3. It refers to the fact that we can do things by "figuring things out," by calculation, by "instrumental reasoning" (e.g., game theory).

        4. It refers to having the right goals as well as adopting the right means to reach them (e.g., Aristotle's claim that reason helps us to want the right things).

    B. Socrates "turns reason into a tyrant," by treating reason as the royal road to truth.

        1. He uses it to refute the half-baked beliefs of his contemporaries.

        2. He argues for an absolute set of standards that are comprehensible by reason alone.

C. The eighteenth century Enlightenment renewed the priority of reason.

   1. The Enlightenment was opposed to the medieval notion of *faith*. It had its own faith, faith in science and reason to solve our problems.

   2. Kant considered religious faith to be necessary.

   3. But most Enlightenment thinkers opposed traditional religious faith.

   4. Some Enlightenment philosophers emphasized sentiment, but not the passions.

   5. The Enlightenment stressed the Apollonian over the Dionysian.

   6. The Enlightenment was inherently universalist.

D. The Enlightenment had a problematic reception in Germany. Romanticism was dominant in Germany.

   1. Romanticism, as a set of tendencies, can be traced back to ancient times.

   2. Jean-Jacques Rousseau was a powerful influence on German Romanticism. So were the British thinkers David Hume and Adam Smith, who developed theories of the sentiments.

   3. In Germany, the Enlightenment was considered vulgar (e.g., by Hegel and Schopenhauer).

   4. The Romantics put their faith not in reason, but in the passions.

II. Nietzsche shocks philosophers by emphasizing the importance of drives and instincts in human behavior. This has become more commonplace since Freud, but it is a precocious recognition of unconscious and non-rational motives in the midst of the rationalist Enlightenment.

A. Nietzsche insists that we can find our life's meaning in our instincts and drives, what we share with other animals.

   1. This reflects Darwin's influence on Nietzsche.

   2. This also links Nietzsche with Freud.

B. Nietzsche anticipates the Unconscious.

   1. Freud later writes, "philosophers before me discovered the Unconscious."

   2. Nietzsche claimed that consciousness originated because of our need to communicate with others.

3. Nietzsche (more than Freud) argues that consciousness is dispensable. As individuals, we each have our own instincts.
4. Conscious thought can blind us to our own creativity. Thinking and consciousness are dangerous.
5. However, perhaps consciousness can play a more positive role at a later stage of human development.

C. Nietzsche's emphasis on the importance of the passions and his diminution of reason links him to Romanticism.
 1. Nietzsche, like the Romantics, praised the passions and the irrational.
 2. But Nietzsche, like the great poet Goethe, finds romanticism "sickly" and shallow. ("They muddy the waters to make them look deep.")

D. Nietzsche comes to see that the passions should not be sharply opposed to reason, but rather both include and encompass reason.
 1. He writes, "as if every passion did not include its quantum of reason."
 2. He suggests that reason is nothing but a confluence of the passions.

Essential Reading:

"Art and Aesthetics" in R. J. Hollingdale, ed., *A Nietzsche Reader*, pp. 125–148.

Twilight of the Idols, "'Reason' in Philosophy," "Morality as Anti-Nature," and "Four Great Errors."

Supplemental Reading:

Richard Schacht, "Nietzsche's Kind of Philosophy" in *Cambridge Companion*, pp. 151–179.

Robert C. Solomon, "100 Years of *Ressentiment*" in Richard Schacht, ed., *Nietzsche: Selections*; *Genealogy, Morality*, especially pp. 102–106.

Questions to Consider:

1. Can a person be *too* rational? What does this mean?
2. The passions are often said to be irrational and destructive, even a bit of insanity. Is there a fair evaluation of the passions?

Lecture Nine—Transcript
Nietzsche on Reason, Instinct, and Passion

I did an earlier lecture by noting very quickly that, if there is a meaning of life for Nietzsche, it is to be found not in reason and rationality but, rather, in the passions. What I would like to do in this lecture is to spell that thesis out in much more detail.

Perhaps the first thing to say is that, if you look at the Western tradition in philosophy—and this includes, I would say, a good deal of the philosophy that is going on in the English-speaking world today—philosophy is all about reason and rationality, and, although philosophers are often a bit contemptuous of the undergraduate question, "What is the meaning of life?" nevertheless, they would hold out that, if that question has an answer, it is to be gained only through the use of reason. One can trace that certainly back to Socrates and perhaps before. Socrates was adamant about the fact that, for example, we should not yield to our emotions. That's what he says to Crito in the midst of one of the most famous early dialogues, that reason is the way to save your soul and reason is the way to find the truth.

In medieval philosophy, reason was often equated with God himself. In modern philosophy, for example in the Enlightenment, reason now equated with science was considered the way to answer all human problems and the way to know about the world, and, in contemporary philosophy, it's often said that philosophy has been reduced to or certainly focuses on pure logic—reason pure and simple—and appeal to emotions is simply out of place. But the first thing to notice about rationality is that it doesn't have a single meaning, that in the history of philosophy it takes on a number of different masks and they don't always go together completely nicely.

First, you might notice that rationality, certainly as most philosophers talk about it, refers to the general class of activities such as thinking, the ability to reflect, the ability to use a fairly sophisticated kind of language, and, as a very general feature, one might say that rationality is to that extent a faculty that humans certainly possess, almost all of us—and perhaps some higher animals possess to a lesser degree—but it's the ability to use concepts and, with concepts, the ability to understand the world in something more than simply stimulus response patterns.

Then there's a much more sophisticated but also much more narrow use of the notion of rationality. The ancient Greeks sum this up in terms of mathematics. It is said that, on the walls of Plato's academy, it said, basically, "If you don't know geometry, don't come in." Bertrand Russell sums up this view of rationality in the Greeks by saying, rather whimsically, "The Greeks thought that we were rational because we could do sums." There is another meaning of rationality that is broader: it is a kind of instrumental reasoning, to use the language that became popular at the beginning of this century. It's to think in means, ends, terms. It's rationality now as a kind of practical, even a kind of strategic, faculty.

In fact, there is a good deal of contemporary philosophy, ethics so-called, in which one of the models is what is called game theory, and you think your way, you reason your way through the best way to achieve your goals and, in particular, the best way to achieve your goals against an opponent. That's a use of the word rationality, and, of course, there we are starting to get into some rather gray territory.

Finally, rationality has to do with not the way to achieve your goals or the best way of competing with an opponent, but rationality has to do with having the right goals, and with this we go back to the Greeks again. Aristotle, for example, never would have allowed that reason is simply, as modern thinkers have argued, a way of figuring out how to get what you want. Reason is, at least in part, wanting the right things. So there is a sense in which, if you look just at these four meanings, you already get a sense of quite a wide spread from the abstractness and impracticality, in one sense, of pure mathematics to the, I think, obsessive, strategic rationality of something like game theory and trying to figure out how to beat your opponent.

But there is another meaning of rationality that runs through the history of philosophy. It is perhaps most clear in Plato and in Socrates, but it continues through certainly the twentieth century. You find it, for example, in some of the European phenomenologists at the beginning of this century, and you still find it in some analytic philosophers in England and America. Basically, it's the notion that reason is the royal road to the truth, that reason doesn't just allow us to perceive—and philosophers have been in agreement since ancient times—that sometimes our experience can be misleading but reason somehow bypasses all that. In someone like Kant, for example, reason allows us to make some sort of contact with the world in itself, the world as it really is.

Socrates, perhaps the luminary figure in all this, had a concept that he shared with several of his Greek colleagues. It's the concept of nous, which is generally translated as something like intellectual intuition. But if you remember that story that both Kathy and I have now told, "The Myth of the Cave," in which the slave who has seen only shadows emerges into the sunlight and then returns to tell his fellows what he has seen, that image of seeing reality through the shadows of everyday experience, that is nous; it is reason as a special facility to directly see the truth, even if as mortals we can only get a glimpse of it now and then.

Socrates takes this notion of reason together with some of the other notions of reason—reason as thinking, reason as reflecting, reason as the skillful use of language—and turns it into a method. It's part of what he means by dialectic, but the basic idea is that, for Socrates, this kind of reasoning process, which, as I emphasized, is for him very much a social process—this is the way to gain the truth. Again he excludes the emotions, the passions; he excludes public opinion. In Nietzsche's words, what Socrates does is he turns reason into a tyrant so that it becomes the only mode of philosophical thinking, and, of course, this is something that is picked up and carried through the twentieth century.

In the Enlightenment, which is roughly the seventeenth through nineteenth centuries, it spread through Europe from west to east. It was in England first; then it got to France; then it hit Germany fairly late, and, with a mixed reception, it finally reached Russia about the beginning of this century and resulted in a revolution there as it had in France earlier. Of course, it reached America right from its inception in the eighteenth century. The Enlightenment, as it's usually characterized, is basically a kind of faith, and, of course, some of its critics would say it really is a religious faith, but, in any case, it's a faith. It's faith in reason. Reason as science will solve our problems. Reason as science will allow us to gain knowledge of the world. Reason as practical knowledge will allow us to design the right kinds of societies, to raise people the right way, to improve our educational institutions, or what some conservative critics today would call social engineering. That's very much an Enlightenment concept, and the basic idea is that it is proceeding by way of reason.

This isn't to say that some of the Enlightenment philosophers didn't put a fairly heavy emphasis on what they called sentiment, in particular, the sentiment of sympathy and the kind of sentiments that go into community feeling and living together, but they were by no means advocates of or apologists for what I would call the passions—those very strong, almost maniacal feelings that Nietzsche characterized as the Dionysian. So, in a way, there is a sense in which the Enlightenment is very much opposed to Nietzsche, that the Apollonian in its strict form from Socrates through the Enlightenment is really the contrast to the Dionysian. It also is opposed to a certain kind of faith.

Now, there is an interesting argument that goes on here between, for example, those who think of faith as a kind of passionate commitment and, most notably, I think, Soren Kierkegaard, the Danish existentialist and religious thinker, and those who actually take faith and even move it into the rationalist camp. For example, Kant defines a notion of faith in which faith isn't mere belief, much less believing what all the evidence says the other way. To the contrary, faith is a mode of reason; faith is a kind of postulate of our moral attitudes, and if you accept morality, as a rational person must, then you must also accept, almost by sheer logic, the necessity of religious faith, too. But what's very interesting there is that the Enlightenment, of which Kant is the primary German representative, is so adamant about the exclusivity of reason that even religion has to be brought into the umbrella of reason and not left in the obscure, murky realm of emotion.

One of the pretensions of reason is that it is universal, and that's, of course, one of the things that Kant finds most important about it because, when you reason, you reason not just for yourself, and when you reason, you are not simply reflecting the beliefs or even the language of your particular culture. When you reason, you are reasoning not only for all of humanity, but Kant expands it even further so that you reason for all rational creatures, and that, of course, would include God as well as angels and any other rational beings that might exist in the universe apart from human beings. What follows from this is that God is a rational being, and that equation that comes out of the Middle Ages of God and reason starts to make perfectly good sense. God commands what He does, God has created what He has created not because He loved the world so much as because He reasoned that this is the right thing to do, for God.

The Enlightenment had a problematic reception in Germany because, although Kant was a very enthusiastic advocate there is a sense—funny sense—in which Kant is more an English or a French philosopher than a German one because the dominant mode of thought in Germany was what we now call Romanticism. Romanticism also has a very interesting history. Part of the interest is that it is almost coincidental with the Enlightenment. It, too, begins in England and moves through France to Germany, but, in Germany, it's the dominant mode of thought. Now Romanticism, although the concept itself is very modern, can also be traced back to ancient times. One might say, for example, that the Dionysian cults were Romantic in a sense, and certainly all of those authors, say, St. Augustine, who put their emphasis on faith and faith not in a necessarily rational sense, could also be considered proto-Romantics.

The dominant Romantic of modern times, the one who in many ways set the entire movement in motion was the Swiss-French philosopher Jean-Jacques Rousseau, who, in particular, emphasized the importance of the sentiments and the implication, at least, of the emotions as opposed to pure reason. Along with him, interestingly enough, David Hume in Scotland and his best friend Adam Smith also defended the sentiments and minimized the importance of reason in our moral sensibilities. But, in Germany, Romanticism took on a stark contrast with the Enlightenment. Hume, for example, or Rousseau—both would have considered themselves Enlightenment philosophers. But, in Germany, the Enlightenment was generally considered vulgar, and it was associated at that time with the alien cultures of England and France.

Hegel, for example, treats the Enlightenment very dismissively in his books, although one could argue that Hegel was very much the heir of the Enlightenment as the student of Kant. Schopenhauer could very nicely be called a Romantic philosopher, and he was certainly treated that way by a good many of the young poets and literary people in Germany because he quite directly confronted the Enlightenment, the idea that reason will make life better for us, and rejected it. In brief, the idea is that the Romantics, as opposed to the Enlightenment thinkers, didn't put their faith in reason but put it somewhere else, and that somewhere else, I think, can best be described as the passions.

Now, in Schopenhauer, this is perhaps the most distinct because, in Schopenhauer, if I can translate what we have been talking about as the will and experiencing the will in us and generalize that, what one might say is that what Schopenhauer says is, what's real, or a contact with what's really real, are our passions, and sexual passion is one example of that. But there is a sense in which a great many of our passions are exemplary of what the world is really about, and what Nietzsche wants to say is that it is in your passions—not in what you think and calculate, not in what's necessarily rational—where you find yourself. That's where you find meaning, and, in particular, that's where you find the meaning of the world.

As Kathy said in a prior lecture, for Nietzsche, seeing the world as an aesthetic phenomenon is not, as it is for Schopenhauer, a way of withdrawing from it, but, rather, it's a way of engaging with it, and so, for Nietzsche, the idea is that aesthetics is extremely important, as it was for Schopenhauer, but aesthetics is important, in a way, for exactly the opposite reason because to see things as beautiful, to see yourself as beautiful, to live your life, to make it beautiful—that's all a way of engaging with the world. It's a way of putting you into the flow of life as opposed to removing yourself one step from it. With that in mind, one has to understand that Nietzsche is doing something very shocking in the history of philosophy. Not that it's the first time that it has ever been done. In fact, he has some German predecessors.

But, as opposed to this very strong emphasis that the Enlightenment endorsed one's reason as the sole road to truth, Nietzsche accepts a very different picture. It's one that's hinted at by Kant at the beginning of one of his works where he talks about God creating us like the animals with instincts and so on, but he also gave us something more, which is what makes us distinctively human, and that is reason. But, of course, then Kant goes on to talk only about reason. What Nietzsche does, by contrast, is he emphasizes the extent to which reason, in fact, is kind of superfluous. Kant says something like, "If the purpose of life was to be happy, God would have put in us simple instinct because, after all, most animals live fairly good lives, and they do it not by thinking their way through it, not by appreciating what life is all about, but just by following their instincts, and, to tell you the truth, if people just followed their instincts, there would probably be fewer wars, fewer conflicts. We would get along much better because we would have much less sophisticated desires; the notion of private property, for example, wouldn't come into question. But, of course, that's not the way we are."

What Nietzsche wants to say is that, if we are going to talk about trusting our instincts at all, we should take that very seriously. So one of the moves that Nietzsche makes, again, might be thought of as a shift from philosophy in the abstract, rather ethereal conceptual sense to the nitty-gritty of biology. It's another example of his naturalism, another example of his this-worldliness. It's another example of how much he is very close to Darwin, although he has a great deal to say against Darwin as well. He says that we are animals. We are motivated primarily by drives, by instincts, by an inborn capacity.

Nietzsche would not have known about genetics at this point, but, basically, it is very clear that what we are as a species, what we are as individuals is something that is very much natural, biological, part of our makeup, and so, instead of those philosophers who want to say the meaning of life is to be found in the higher reaches of reason, Nietzsche wants to say the meaning of life is to be found in life itself and the instincts that we find in ourselves are not ours uniquely as human beings but in conjunction with the rest of the animals.

The idea that it's instinct and drive that moves us and gives us meaning is another one of those very important links to Sigmund Freud, who will be writing only a decade later. Freud, of course, talks about the unconscious, and, in particular, he also uses a great deal of drive language. The idea is that the things that really move us, the things that determine our lives, are not things that we are fully conscious of, and, given the nature of many of those urges and desires as Freud describes them, it's a good thing we are not conscious of them, and, in fact, it's only when they lead us into serious trouble that it's a good thing to become fully conscious of them.

There's always this sort of dual role of Freud's philosophy, if I can call that. On the one hand, it's very important to become conscious of what's going on in the unconscious in order to control it, in order to move beyond it. At the same time, there is a sense in which we can't do that, and the forces of repression are so necessary for civilization that there is a sense in which understanding it not only doesn't do any good but, to the contrary, just makes us more unhappy. With Nietzsche, consciousness is itself dispensable. In one of the most striking passages in *Gay Science*—in fact, I think it's just about the longest single passage in *The Gay Science*—Nietzsche talks about consciousness and asks the question, one that Freud actually doesn't ask, of where it comes from.

It's a very important question, and Nietzsche has a theory. Consciousness is a faculty that has developed in us because of the necessity of communication. Now, we often think—and certainly since Descartes in the seventeenth century it's a central part of philosophy—that each of us has a mind and that mind is almost by definition conscious and self-conscious as well, and, in the mind, we find thoughts as well as feelings, and then we communicate those, with some trouble, perhaps, through language to other people.

Nietzsche has the opposite view. Consciousness is actually created in our interaction, in our communication with others. But also, insofar as Nietzsche is defending a view of human existence not as a herd existence or, less unflatteringly, not as a social existence, necessarily, he is defending a kind of ferocious individualism that we will talk about later. One might say that, insofar as one can live solitudinously, consciousness in a way becomes superfluous. The truth is if we follow our instincts—and instinct here, by the way, is not simply the primitive birdlike instinct to build a nest and not simply the primitive doglike instinct to attack a male rival, but rather very sophisticated notions of instincts. For example, there are aesthetic instincts, and Nietzsche thinks that this is something very basic.

Leaving aside the question of to what extent these might be culturally derived or genetically derived, what's clear for Nietzsche is that we have all sorts of instincts that, in fact, are very sophisticated and very cultured, and, most important, they're very individual. As we will see, Nietzsche is going to talk about the virtues, Nietzsche's going to talk about the emotions, Nietzsche is going to talk about the grand passions in such a way that they are very distinctively each our own.

It's, in a way, the opposite of Schopenhauer where these things really are what hold us together as a larger unity, and it's even opposed to one sense of the Dionysian, at least the Dionysian writ large, where passion is something that holds us all together. That's true insofar as we are talking about something like a Dionysian orgy, but the truth is that, for the purposes that Nietzsche wants in philosophy and in aesthetics, what's important is that each of us has his or her own instincts, and to even give them a name, for example, to call it territorial imperative, or to call it the creative spirit is already, in a sense, to make it sound more common.

So Nietzsche's view on consciousness here is something very complicated and something that, unfortunately, he doesn't work out in a great deal of detail, but the simple message is that thinking can even be a disease. Thinking can be dangerous, and not dangerous in a good sense. It's dangerous in a sense that it shuts us down, it inhibits us, it blinds us to our own particularities, our own uniqueness, our own creativity. He says, as do Kierkegaard and Dostoevsky about the same time, that quite the contrary of consciousness being the high point, the pinnacle of human facilities, consciousness is dangerous. But, as so often with Nietzsche, what he attacks he also brings back by a back route because consciousness is a very important stage in our evolution.

He says that whenever a faculty is new it is something that is so far untried, something in which we are unskilled, something that we will abuse, and, consequently, something that is dangerous for survival. But, as it matures, as we get better at it, then, of course, consciousness can play a much more positive role, and one can look at Nietzsche's own thought and writing as exemplary here. He is one of the masters of language, German language in particular, but I would say, insofar as you can make these comparisons, he is one of the masters of language in the human history. But the idea here is that language is now still kind of finding its feet; that's why Nietzsche is so experimental with it. How does language capture the truth? How does language capture human nature? How does language in particular capture what for each of us is the meaning of life?

Now, this makes Nietzsche very much in line with the Romantics, but it's important to sort of point out that, just as Nietzsche often attacks figures who would seem to be fairly close to him, Socrates being the most obvious example, he also attacks movements that would seem to be very much his own, but he says of Romanticism, in one of his more sarcastic comments, that Romanticism muddies the waters to make them look deep, and he is very critical of many of the Romantic poets and philosophers of his time for trying to sound profound when, in fact, they are really just uttering platitudes, or what they are doing is making kind of cosmic statements.

Of course, Schopenhauer falls into this category, some sense of the world sweeping through us and so on, and one can kind of envision this in two different ways: if you know the paintings of Caspar Friedrich, you know that typically he will have a lone individual in some majestic scene in which the landscape is sort of covered by fog and there are mountains in the background and all sorts of interesting shadows, and you get the sense of the individual kind of lost in nature. Or a different kind of depiction is Wagner's overtures. My favorite is the "Overture to the Flying Dutchman," in which you get this musical rendition where you really feel yourself sort of swirling through space and time. But, ultimately, Nietzsche wants to say that's not the right view either.

Romanticism, as Goethe had put it before him, has a very strong tendency to be sickly. In fact, it's a kind of pretended passion. Instead of expressing the passions, the instincts, the drives that are really within us—and very powerful at that—what Romanticism does is it manufactures them. It makes them look as if they are grand passions when, in fact, they're really just poetic aspirations or perhaps just the desire to sort of fit in with the new Romantic crowd, in other words, the same kind of criticism he levels at Christianity, the same kind of criticism he levels at the moral majority—that, basically, this presents itself as something cosmic and essentially important, but, in fact, it's a kind of mask, it's a kind of act.

Although I have been using the distinction between reason and passion and talking as if reason and passion are opposed in the Enlightenment, in Romanticism, and so on, Nietzsche's view, I think, is, in fact, much more interesting and much more sophisticated. The truth is these are not distinct at all. He writes, in one place, "as if every passion doesn't contain its quantum of reason," and elsewhere he suggests that reason is nothing but the confluence of the passions. So the picture here is that, when we are talking about the human spirit, what we are really talking about is something that is intrinsically passionate and intrinsically rational, in other words, the combination of the Apollonian and the Dinonysian.

Lecture Ten
Nietzsche's Style and the Problem of Truth

Scope:

What is most striking about reading Nietzsche, before one even gets to the polemics, is his famous style. He often writes in aphorisms, small explosions of insight without explanation. He uses as many exclamation points, emphatic italics and "scare quotes" as a *Glamour* magazine journalist. Against every canon of "logical correctness," Nietzsche makes extensive use of *ad hominem* arguments, arguments directed against the person rather than the thesis or the argument. He also appeals to emotion, another form of fallacious argument. Perhaps it is not surprising, given Nietzsche's denigration of reason and his fallacious arguing, that he has skeptical views about the central philosophical notion of *truth*.

Outline

I. Nietzsche's style is experimental, shifting from eccentric classical scholarship to aphoristic to Biblical parody to polemic essay and mock autobiography.

  A. These experiments complicate interpretation of his works. Their purpose is to incite our own thought, and to shock us into a different way of seeing things.

    1. For example, Nietzsche sometimes utilizes fictional characters, such as one of Zarathustra's interlocutors, the "Ugliest Man."

    2. The Ugliest Man claims to have killed God.

    3. This is a playful image that tells a story; it is not presented as an assertion. Instead, it is suggestive.

  B. Nietzsche employs "musical" characteristics of writing, such as tempo.

  C. The strategy of the aphorism is to provoke thought. Nietzsche wants his readers to be active.

    1. For example, consider the famous aphorism "*Out of life's school of war. What does not destroy me, makes me stronger.*"

2. This can mean many different things. Nietzsche does not tell us which possible meaning he endorses, or whether he endorses more than one.

II. Nietzsche often employs what most philosophers would consider fallacies, classic examples of bad arguments.

   A. In particular, he uses *ad hominem* arguments.
   1. An *ad hominem* argument is personal and aimed at the person.
   2. It is unlike "respectable" philosophical arguments, which are impersonal and concern only the logic of the argument.

   B. He also employs "appeals to emotion." Whereas most philosophers follow Socrates in insisting that we should not be swayed by our passions. Nietzsche writes with such passion.

III. If Nietzsche is so skilled at rhetoric, what happens to the truth?

   A. We need to consider that argument is a form of art.
   1. Many deductive arguments lack persuasive power.
   2. Philosophy is not logic but rhetoric.
   3. Many of Socrates' arguments are logically bad, but powerful for other reasons.
   4. Nietzsche is doing art, not science.

   B. The question of rhetoric's relation to truth is a question that Socrates raised against the Sophists, but Nietzsche's answer is even more radical. Nietzsche says, "There is no truth; there are only interpretations."

IV. Like most intellectuals in the late nineteenth century, Nietzsche was fascinated with and knowledgeable about science. Sometimes he even praised his own work as "most scientific."

   A. Nietzsche's views about science display a number of variations.
   1. He sometimes views science as essentially experimental, and in this sense he has considerable admiration for it. He wants to experiment with ideas, just as scientists experiment.
   2. He also views science as naturalistic, which is not to say materialistic, but opposed to any explanations that

invoke the supernatural. With this, too, he is obviously in agreement.

3. He sometimes praises science for its non-dogmatic nature, the fact that no conclusion is final, the door to new evidence and new hypotheses and theories is always open. Our knowledge of the world is always tentative. Again, Nietzsche registers nothing but approval.

4. Sometimes, especially early in his work, he opposes science to an aesthetic view of the world. Only occasionally does he identify the two, as many scientists would, in finding aesthetic beauty in understanding how the world works.

B. Later in his career, he turns against science.

1. He accuses science of being ascetic, a form of self-denial, an obsession with truth to the detriment of life. His fellow scholars were obviously included in this indictment.

2. When science becomes dogmatic, it loses its virtue.

3. Nietzsche also comes to identify science with positivism, an exclusive emphasis on the facts. But since he insists that "there are no facts," this conception of science is obviously inadequate.

Essential Reading:

Nietzsche, *Twilight of the Idols*, "The Problem of Socrates."

"Truth and Lies in an Extra-Moral Sense," in Richard Schacht, ed., *Nietzsche: Selections*.

Supplemental Reading:

Alexander Nehemas, *Nietzsche*, Chapter 1.

Robert C. Solomon, "Nietzsche *Ad Hominem*" in *Cambridge Companion*, pp. 180–222.

Questions to Consider:

1. Can rhetoric show us the way to the truth? Why does Nietzsche so prefer rhetorical devices (overstatement, personal insults) to the standard philosophical logic and argumentation?

2. Can an *ad hominem* argument in fact throw light on a philosophical thesis? Can calling Socrates "ugly" show us anything whatsoever about his philosophy?

Lecture Ten—Transcript
Nietzsche's Style and the Problem of Truth

Higgins: In this lecture we are going to talk about Nietzsche's various literary styles and the implications these have for his quest for truth or, in general, the quest for truth. Nietzsche was an experimentalist with regard to style, and this makes interpreting him a very difficult matter. For example, I have already talked to a great extent about Zarathustra as a character, but I haven't mentioned the fact that other characters sometimes appear in the book about Zarathustra, sometimes there as kind of walk-on parts that are never seen again. One I'll mention because it's of particular interest is a character called "the ugliest man."

Zarathustra encounters a pretty miserable character, who really doesn't want to be seen at all, known as the ugliest man, and eventually gets the ugliest man to confess that he actually is the killer of God. It's hard to know what to make of that, especially when you reflect on the fact that, after all, Socrates is well-known for being ugly. Is Socrates the ugliest man? One might say that Socrates' tradition, in a way, doesn't ally as easily as many people have thought with the Christian tradition. After all, Socrates encourages rational investigation, and that, as Nietzsche sees it, is exactly one of the things that have led to the demise of faith in the Christian God.

On the other hand, one of the comments the ugliest man—the character—makes is that he couldn't stand it any more. God was watching him constantly, and, because he was ugly, it was just something that became intolerable; hence, his motivation. That sounds sort of playful, but again this resonates with the way Nietzsche thinks the death of God has actually come about. More and more, in his opinion, people came to see themselves as fundamentally flawed, fundamentally ugly, fundamentally sinful, and, pushing that to it's extreme point, it becomes intolerable to imagine a divine being viewing all of that; hence, the death of God.

A lot of these rather playful images actually do tell stories or make points that Nietzsche wants to assert, but he doesn't present them as simple assertions, simple statements of the facts of the matter. Instead, they are provocative. In general, I would say, one of his general tendencies or, basically, what he is trying to do is give us an experience of thought, not so much the general idea that he concluded. Many philosophers make arguments defending a certain point and make no effort to explain how it is they came to the conclusion. In fact, truth be told, as Nietzsche sees it, oftentimes philosophers come to their conclusions before constructing the arguments and then only after the fact manufacture arguments that might lead to this conclusion.

In a sense, Nietzsche does the opposite. He starts forays of thought that allow the reader to come to conclusions themselves. Sometimes he pursues them for only a paragraph or a few sentences, sometimes for several pages, and, in the aphoristic works, at least, oftentimes, after pursuing a line of thought, he drops it. Maybe he will pick it up again in a later passage, maybe not. Maybe what he pursues after that seems to be a thought in a very different direction, and, again, I think what he is trying to do is demonstrate something like the process of thinking, that when one has a kind of insight or intuition one does pursue a certain train of thought for a way but then put it down sometimes, maybe never to return to it.

Another aspect of the process of thinking that Nietzsche is concerned with is something that he categorizes as musical. He prides himself on exploring different kinds of tempo, or tempi, in writing, much as a musician might do in music. So he suggests that he has arranged many of his books with a kind of sense of pace in mind. Sometimes he will have a rather plodding pace, attempting to reach a conclusion only very slowly but methodically; other times he allows a kind of gallop to happen so that one is almost breathless by the end of one of his running passages. Again, there is a kind of sense that this is much the way people actually do think, and he isn't so concerned that we draw exactly the conclusions he does as that we share the experience with him to a certain point.

One of the particular stylistic features that we have talked a bit about, but I would like to go into a bit further here, is this use of the aphorism. What are called aphorisms in Nietzsche's works, as we have mentioned, sometimes extend for several pages, but the quintessential aphorism is essentially a simple line. And Nietzsche has a lot to say about his reliance on the aphorism. He describes it as something like stepping from mountaintop to mountaintop, and he makes it very clear that he doesn't think the reader is going to get the whole story simply by reading the aphorism. What the aphorism has to do with is Nietzsche's desire for an active readership, not people who passively go along with what he says and simply draw the same conclusions that he does but, instead, fellow companions in thought who engage the same kind of train of thought to an extent but then are free to pursue it any way they like. Indeed, Nietzsche wants companions in this respect, not simple followers.

I am going to take an example of one of Nietzsche's aphorisms and suggest the many ways in which one might continue the line of thought just to point out how variably one might take it, and this is probably one of his most famous aphorisms—actually even heard in such popular culture venues as *Conan the Barbarian*, the particular line being, "What doesn't kill me makes me stronger." Actually, this line, although quoted oftentimes out of context without attribution, is not simply that line as quoted, but it has a preface as Nietzsche states it. The preface is, "Out of life's school of war." "Out of life's school of war: What doesn't kill me, makes me stronger."

I think with the preface we are given certain suggestions as to how we might take it, but very, very different directions might emerge. For example, you might see this as a suggestion that life is rough, it is a bit like a school of war, and, in a sense, what doesn't kill me makes me stronger. You almost have to think that if you are going to get through it alive. On the other hand, maybe it's simply the reversal that Nietzsche is getting at. Out of life's school of war, what doesn't kill me makes me stronger. Well, in a certain straightforward way, thinking about military thought, there is a sense in which defeats actually do take a toll. What doesn't kill you might, in fact, make you a lot more vulnerable toward the future. So we get a reversal of what's expected here. What could that possibly mean?

Well, perhaps another way of looking at it is to say, what doesn't kill me makes me stronger in that I have learned from experience. In military thinking or in any kind of strategic thinking in life, having certain kinds of experiences makes you more prepared for what you might come across in the future, even though it probably won't be identical. So you are stronger in that you are more prepared—you're readied. But what are you ready for? Perhaps this isn't just a kind of whistling in the dark of someone who realizes that they might be risking their life in this case. What doesn't kill me makes me stronger in the sense that I'm not going to let it get me down.

Then there is the psychological impact, and this, I think, makes particularly good sense if you think about this in the context of an actual war. What doesn't kill me makes me stronger. Suppose I haven't been killed despite all kinds of situations that might have threatened me. In that case, what's the enemy going to think? It's going to be a lot like a team playing a team that's undefeated for the season. They haven't been killed yet—what makes me, the opponent team, think I can do anything? We get the impression that it's a psychological advantage to have been through a lot and still manage to face battle in the future. This is a great psychological advantage by comparison to someone who, perhaps, is untested. It's always terrifying to face, as an opponent, someone who is thought very highly of, who is viewed as strong.

Or, perhaps what Nietzsche is getting at is that we end up developing a kind of suit of armor by virtue of our experiences. We become hardened, in a sense. We aren't the vulnerable individual that we start out being, but, instead, through life's school of war, we have learned to, in effect, become our own armor or make a kind of armor out of our skin that makes us less sensitive, but, on the other hand, we are certainly stronger.

I point to all these possible ways of reading the line in order to draw attention to the fact that Nietzsche doesn't tell us which, if any of them, he has in mind himself. He simply drops this as a line for our further thinking. And, in general, I think many of his stylistic experiments attempt to do the same. One of his strategies that often occurs in the aphoristic works is that he juxtaposes things. In *Day Break* or *Dawn*, for instance, he has a series of passages that open the work that talk a lot about custom—how certain habits for societies simply become customary after a point. When he talks about this, you get the impression that he is perhaps going to launch a kind of anthropological investigation. Suddenly he, in a sense, shifts topics by talking about morality, and it seems that he has sort of opened up a totally new line of thought.

I think subtly what he is trying to suggest is this really isn't a totally new line of thought, that if you think about customs and habits and then think about morality, are they really entirely different things? He would say that our moralities are really entrenched customs, customs that our societies take to be particularly important, perhaps, but really exactly the same thing, having the same status—certain ways of being that people have found useful or merely traditional and stuck by and felt to be important, really, for no other reason fundamentally than the fact that others have done it before them.

Frequently, I think, what he is trying to do is allow these kinds of connections to emerge in our own minds. So, although he does want active readership that is going to move forward in thought and take things further—and, indeed, he often says he doesn't necessarily want to be followed but nevertheless read and grappled with—still, he does sometimes manipulate. So it would be rather surprising if, after all this discussion of habit and custom, one didn't end up thinking, "Hmm, isn't he possibly suggesting that this is a habit too, that our mores are really simply traditions, habits—and, I think, the big point—changeable?"

Solomon: Reading Nietzsche, it becomes obvious that he doesn't follow what now is considered the standard philosophical mode, and Kathy's account of aphoristic thinking in particular makes the why of this very clear. The dominant mode, at least since Descartes with the rise of science in the West, has been that philosophy is essentially an argument and, in particular, it's a kind of deduction. Now, there are philosophers who deviate from this. For example, they would say it's partly an inductive argument, an argument based on experience. Nevertheless, this notion of an argument, something that proceeds from evidence or premise to conclusion—methodically—is something that has dominated the Western tradition for the last 300 years.

The most famous example here of course, is Descartes, who, quite explicitly, modeled his philosophical method on geometry. Perhaps slightly less known, but equally luminary in the early modern philosophy is the Dutch philosopher Spinoza, who said, in effect, that truth must be expressed in a geometrical deductive style, and to read Spinoza's *View on Ethics*, which, in fact, is a very sensitive, personal book, talking about things like fate and feeling and faith, the truth is, you open it up, and it looks like a geometry textbook with propositions and theorems and corollaries and QED's, and even people like Kant, he calls one of the primary chapters in his greatest book "A Deduction." Some of the Romantics and some of the philosophers of the early nineteenth century who were clearly not in the strictly Enlightenment camp also refer to what they are doing as deduction.

And, of course, the English all the way through, notably, John Stuart Mill, who is first of all a logician—that's what his philosophy is centered on—and contemporary American English philosophy, as we all know, is very centered on formal logical arguments. Not Nietzsche. In fact, one might say that, by this criterion, a criterion that philosophy consists of an argument, a kind of deduction, that all of Nietzsche really consists of a sequence of fallacies, that, basically, it's all a matter of not doing philosophy right or, as many people would put it, not doing philosophy at all but, rather, doing some sort of literature, some sort of rhetoric, some sort of art form—but not philosophy.

We have already discussed in some detail the sense in which Nietzsche, for example, employs ad hominem arguments, in which he attacks the person rather than the thesis or the argument. The purpose behind this is essentially to give us a larger picture. It's not just the argument, it's not just the inference, and it's not just the conclusion, but, rather, it's the whole package of the philosopher and his or her philosophy, and, of course, his or her world, the circumstances that give rise to it, and, as we suggested, this is fair turnabout to turn on Nietzsche and say that Nietzsche has to be considered, not just in terms of his ideas and his conclusions but also in terms of his life, and, in particular, his incredible solitude, his continuous illness, the brevity of his life.

It's an ad hominem argument, but Nietzsche would say it's only such ad hominem arguments that allow us to get the full picture of what's going on in philosophy. And so, too, we suggested that Nietzsche—contrary to the reigning philosophical style going back to Socrates, in this case—often appeals to emotion, and he makes no bones about it. He makes it very clear, as did Kierkegaard before him, that what he is doing is trying to stimulate what Kathy referred to as our experience and in particular our emotional experience, to make us disgusted often with ourselves, to make us curious about the world, to make us see beauty where perhaps we didn't see it before, and, in Kierkegaard's case, of course, to prod us into faith where before we had perhaps been too timid to try it.

But appeals to emotion for Nietzsche and for Kierkegaard are the absolute essence of philosophy. One might say that, for Nietzsche—trying to prod us into these emotional experiences—philosophy becomes, in the dichotomy that's been around since Plato, a matter of rhetoric, not a matter of logic and argument.

Now, I mentioned in a previous lecture that Socrates, although he himself distinguished his work from those of his rivals, the Sophists, and Plato certainly makes this very clear, I suggested that, in fact, Socrates really is one of the Sophists; in fact, he is one of the best of them. The truth is that sophistry, as we now use that term, isn't just a matter of argument, but it's also appeal to emotion, and it is, to put it in terms that Nietzsche would certainly approve, an art form. Argument, after all, is an art form. Philosophers, I think, when they use strict logical form, convince no one. Take, for example, some of the famous arguments that prove God's existence, which Kierkegaard makes fun of at great length. I won't go into the details here, but the idea that, for example, if you can have a thought of an infinite being, that it follows, through some fairly fancy logical footwork, that such a being must exist.

I am willing to bet that there is not a single individual in the history of religion who has ever been converted on the basis of such an argument. Saint Anselm, the most famous Christian thinker who invented one version of that complicated argument, in fact, embeds it within a statement of devout faith and makes it very clear the point of the argument is not conversion—convincing the unbeliever—but, rather, for someone who already believes, this is a kind of rational structure to put on top of the belief. In general, philosophy is not logic; philosophy is a kind of rhetoric, and, of course, Socrates himself was a great rhetorician. Many of his arguments, every classic scholar will agree, are terrible. They really are not even the kind of argument that we would allow in a freshman undergraduate class. Nevertheless, they are very powerful, and they are powerful because of Socrates' personality; they are powerful because of the mode of presentation; they are powerful because he knows how to deal with other people; and so, too, with Nietzsche.

One is not doing him a disservice when one says, as a good many of the postmodernists recently have said, that what he is doing is rhetoric, not logic. I think a better way to put it is that what Nietzsche is doing is art, not science. But that's in a way unfair because Nietzsche often says he is doing science, which raises a very important question. I would put it this way: If what Nietzsche is doing is rhetorical—it's convincing us, appealing to our emotions— then what happens to truth? Because famously rhetoric allows us to convince people of many matters that are not true, and logic doesn't give us any protection. As I said, a logical argument standing against a powerful emotional appeal usually doesn't stand a chance or only, perhaps, with a handful of philosophers.

So what happens to the truth? One of Nietzsche's answers is that it gets lost away, and we have already seen some of the reasons why he says this. I'm going to come back to it in the next lecture and talk about Nietzsche's theories of truth in much more detail. But the dominant view that he presents throughout his philosophy looks like this: There is no truth; there are only interpretations. Now, that sounds very much like a rejection of truth altogether. But then one thinks about something Kathy said in the last lecture about Nietzsche and the importance of truthfulness. Nietzsche was a philosopher who prided himself and praised Zarathustra and Jesus and Socrates for their truthfulness, their willingness to speak the truth even against popular opposition and current tradition.

But what sense does it make to talk about truthfulness, to talk about honesty, to talk about forthrightness if you don't have truth somewhere to go along with it? Well, one way to answer that question and one way of mixing up the categories that I have just been using is to say that Nietzsche clearly sees philosophy as an art form, and his writing is clearly proof of that. It's not antagonistic with science, but, rather, Nietzsche, like most of the other thinkers at the end of the nineteenth century, was fascinated by science, took science very seriously, read what I guess these days would be the German equivalent of *Scientific American*. He knew what was going on and found it fascinating. But science isn't a singular enterprise, either, and just as I discussed regarding rationality, I think it's important to understand that, when Nietzsche and other philosophers talk about science, as when they talk about rationality, they are often referring to different things and consequently have very different attitudes towards them.

Now, early in his career, particularly in the aphoristic period of *Human, All Too Human*, *Daybreak*, and *Gay Science*, Nietzsche prized science and often referred to his work as scientific for one reason above all else. And that is because it was experimental. As Kathy said in the last lecture, Nietzsche's style is through and through experimental. He is trying to have different effects; he is trying different ways of having the desired effect. Science is also experimental; it tries things, and one of Nietzsche's greatest phrases of praise says, "I'm willing to admire any hypothesis which allows, let us try it."

And, of course, this is, as with some of the philosophers of the Enlightenment, Voltaire, for example, a very keen slap in the face against metaphysics and against theology because, after all, there is no evidence that will demonstrate a metaphysical proposition. There is no evidence that would demonstrate the truth of Christianity or any other religion. This is a matter of faith; it's a matter of metaphysics. Perhaps you might say it's a matter of pure reason, but, in any case, it's not something that you can experiment with; it's not something you can look for evidence for, and so Nietzsche wants to say, as Hume did before, let us just dismiss it.

Now, there is another way of thinking about this, of course. You can experiment with religious beliefs, but what you are experimenting with, then, is not the evidence for the proof of God's existence or the Trinity, or anything of the sort. What you are experimenting with— and William James about the same time was writing this out quite explicitly—is the effect of the belief on the believer, and, of course, that's very much in line with what Nietzsche wants to say. But the idea of experimenting with ideas, experimenting with philosophical viewpoints—that's something that he thought was very much a kindred point of view between himself and his philosophy and science.

He also saw science as something purely naturalistic, and to say that science is naturalistic is first of all to say that it's not supernatural or supernaturalistic. Explanations, accounts—whether they are of the behavior of nature or the behavior of human beings—must be couched in the language of science, and that means we have to look for causes and effects, that means we have to look for explanations on the order of biology or chemistry or physics or psychology. It means that it's not good enough to say God created us this way, and you can't get an adequate account of the human mind or psyche by talking about God-given human faculties, as many philosophers and psychologists before him were prone to do.

He also admires science because it's non-dogmatic. Science always leaves itself open, and one of the points that Nietzsche is fond of making, as a great many thinkers today are, if you look back over the history of science and beliefs about the world more generally, the most obvious thing is that most of the beliefs—certainly most of the general theories—that people have held about the world have turned out to be false. The earth is not flat, the earth is not stationary, species are not permanent in nature. Why do we think that our beliefs about science, our current theories, are now true—the arrogance of contemporary popular science? No scientist worthy of his or her title really accepts that. Every scientist knows theories are always tentative, that our so-called knowledge of the world is in place for as long as the evidence holds out and until some anomaly or counter set of evidence outweighs it.

So science is undogmatic, in a very important sense, the same sense in which Nietzsche wants to insist that philosophy should be undogmatic. It is always open to alternatives; it's open to new possibilities; it is open to the idea of plural truths; something we will talk about next time. Sometimes, however, Nietzsche opposes science, and it's a fascinating question in itself to trace throughout his various writings, how these attitudes shift and change. For example, in his very early work, when he is still a classics scholar, fundamentally, there appears to be a kind of opposition with science from an aesthetic point of view. In other words, one might think of the world in terms of nature, science, cause and effect. But, on the other hand, one might think of nature in purely aesthetic terms.

Here is an example. Many years ago, I was sitting with a friend who happens to be a rather accomplished poet in a coffee shop in Austin, and there was a flower on the table. It was a moderately fancy coffee shop, and the flower was perking up through the vase, and my friend said, if I remember more or less correctly, that the flower was spreading its petals and reaching up towards the sun, celebrating the beautiful day. I am an old biologist, and I was remembering back to college and all those lessons I learned about turgor and cell metabolism and tropisms and the like. But I wisely kept my mouth shut because I realized that my explanation of why the flower was stretching its way upward was so much less elegant than his.

There is a sense in which the scientific view of the world can be dry, and, in some of his latest works, *Twilight of the Idols*, in particular, Nietzsche actually takes apart some of the talk about cause and effect, not just in philosophy but even in science more generally, asking whether these concepts are really as specific and as valid as philosophers and scientists assume they are. The aesthetic point of view on the other hand, often invokes images, metaphors, and different kinds of ways of seeing that are distinctively unscientific. And insofar as Nietzsche opposes science and the aesthetic point of view, then it's going to turn out that aesthetics gets the upper hand. But I want to emphasize that this is not usually the case, and often Nietzsche, like a great many contemporary scientists, wants to note the aesthetic value of science itself.

There is something beautiful about seeing how the world works. There is something beautiful, elegant about the right kind of mathematical theory, and one should say that, for Nietzsche, the notion of science is much broader than our notion of science today, that what he was referring to, as were all the prior German philosophers that we have talked about, was Wissenschaft, where I think the more proper way of understanding it might be something like wisdom or discipline, but it's certainly not restricted to the very narrow confines of physical science, which is often the case today. He liked science throughout his career, insofar as science is debunking. He himself—and this is the appeal to Zarathustra and Jesus as well—saw what was important as bucking tradition, sort of popping balloons, exploding old superstitions and traditions, and insofar as science is particularly good at doing, that insofar as science is skeptical, it obviously won Nietzsche's approval.

But, in his very late works, he also turns against science in a different way. Partly, he says, science is not always undogmatic, but sometimes it becomes dogmatic, and, at that point, it loses its virtue, and perhaps more important, he asks the ad hominem question, which I haven't raised so far in this discussion. But the ad hominem question about the scientist himself or herself—and this applies in this Wissenschaft sense, not just to the natural scientist but to the scholar as well—is, Why would people spend their lives often passing up many more pleasurable opportunities just to get the truth? With this, truth itself becomes a serious problem, which we will pick up the next lecture.

Lecture Eleven
Nietzsche on Truth and Interpretation

Scope:

Nietzsche's views on truth and interpretation are not always consistent and he shifted his perspective several times in his career. Early on, he described truth as "a mobile army of metaphors." Later on, he became both enamored with and disappointed with science and the scientific method. He sometimes seems to accept the idea that truth—if there were to be any—would require a match between our beliefs and reality as it is "in itself." Other times he accepted the more modest and consequently more reasonable but relativistic view that truth depends on one's perspective. Nietzsche's "perspectivism" implies that there is no privileged, objective, absolute, or "God's eye" view of the world. The perspectivist view is readily combined with a "pragmatic" view of truth, that truth is disclosed in our serviceable practices and habits rather than in the abstract realm of reason. Truth is interpretation, whether the conscious interpretation of experience (via "the facts") or through the practicalities of what we do.

Outline

I. "There is no truth," "there are no facts," "there are only appearances."

    A. Why is truth important? Why are we interested in it? Why are we willing to pay the costs of attaining truth?

    B. The search for truth can't be isolated; it's part of how we live our lives.

        1. It is bound up with status.

        2. Truth is related to the search for other goals (e.g., "The truth will make you free.").

        3. Truth is a means.

        4. The idea of truth lends itself to a sense of the absolute.

        5. The search for truth is related to the search for power.

II. When Nietzsche claims there is no truth, only interpretations, he suggests that there is no way to get to the bottom of things.

A. We can compare this situation to that of the Bible, which is the product of a series of interpretations. To understand anything is to interpret it.

B. Appearances depend on the things of which they are appearances.
  1. How do you get behind the appearance? This was, for example, Descartes' question.
  2. Kant distinguishes between our experience and the way the world is in itself.

C. Nietzsche claims that when we discard the idea of a "real" world, distinct from the world of appearances, the apparent world also disappears. The distinction is bogus; only our experience exists.

D. When Nietzsche says, "there are no facts," he is not denying the obvious.
  1. He is rather making a point: all facts are already conceived within a language, within a culture, within a perspective, within the constraints and expectations of a theory.
  2. To say that "there are only interpretations" means that there is no non-perspectival, entirely atheoretical view of a "naked" (uninterpreted) state of affairs.

E. When Nietzsche says, "there is no truth," he is not denying that some claims about the world are warranted whereas other are utterly without evidence.
  1. He is making the well-rehearsed philosophical point that we are never in a position to check our perceptions and beliefs against the world "in itself."
  2. All of our checking is within the realm of our experience, noting that some perceptions cohere, others do not; some beliefs follow from one another, others contradict one another.

F. When Nietzsche says, "there are only appearances," he is again making the point that we never encounter the world "in itself."
  1. We can only know the world of our experience.
  2. This is a claim that traces back to Kant and Schopenhauer.

G. The claim that there is no truth leads to paradox.
   1. Is the claim that there is no truth *true*? If so, then it is false.
   2. But this is a misunderstanding of the claim, which is mistakenly presented as a "truth about truth."
   3. It is rather a claim made within the realm of truth, the realm of experience, denying any possible knowledge external to that realm.

H. There is no "God's eye" view of the world.
   1. Even if there were a God, he would have to have a viewpoint.
   2. But then, how does Nietzsche get his distance? He describes the world and his experience not by going outside of them, but rather by moving around rapidly within them.

III. Nietzsche's view of truth might be called "perspectivism."

   A. Perspectivism is just this view that every claim, every experience, every belief, every philosophy, is tied to some perspective.

   B. But there are multiple perspectives, and we can adopt many of them; some with ease (if only we are not dogmatic), others only with difficulty.
      1. There is the possibility of different moral perspectives (for example, Nietzsche distinguishes master and slave morality as two different perspectives on the world).
      2. Perspectivism is not the same thing as relativism; not all perspectives are equal.
      3. The philosopher should adopt as many perspectives as possible, according to Nietzsche. This has led some philosophers to accuse Nietzsche of inconsistency.
      4. Nietzsche avoids committing himself to a single fixed position.

   C. Nietzsche adopts a pragmatic view of truth.
      1. What is philosophical truth? It is understanding how these different perspectives all tie together.
      2. You must be able to hold competing perspectives at the same time.
      3. Nietzsche's view of truth is similar to Darwin's view of fitness.

4. What we believe to be true is just what works in our struggle for survival and self-realization.

Essential Reading:

R. J. Hollingdale, ed., *A Nietzsche Reader*, "Logic, Epistemology, Metaphysics," pp. 53–70.

Nietzsche, *Beyond Good and Evil*, "On the Prejudices of Philosophers," and "The Free Spirit."

Supplemental Reading:

Maudemarie Clark, *Nietzsche on Philosophy and Truth*.

B. Leiter, "Perspectivism in Nietzsche's *Genealogy of Morals*" in Richard Schacht, ed., *Nietzsche: Selections*; *Genealogy, Morality*, pp. 334–357.

Alexander Nehemas, *Nietzsche*, Chapter 2.

Questions to Consider:

1. Nietzsche defends many different views of science as a discipline. Which one(s) do you think is (are) most justified?

2. Nietzsche says "there is no truth." What can he possibly mean by this? Is he right (that is, is his claim *true*)?

Lecture Eleven—Transcript
Nietzsche on Truth and Interpretation

Nietzsche's emphasis on truthfulness and his dedication to science, or Wissenschaft, would suggest that, at the very heart of his endeavor, as at the heart of every scientific or philosophical endeavor, is the pursuit of the truth. But this has to be sort of weighed against Nietzsche's frequent statements, which often go, "There is no truth; there are only interpretations." Or, "There is no truth, only appearances." Or, "There is no truth, only the prejudices of mankind." Or, "There is no truth, only our indispensable errors."

On the one hand, it's very clear that Nietzsche prides himself, above all, as being a truthful philosopher, as talking the world, expressing the world, as he sees it. At the same time, he says, "There is no truth." It's a paradox that runs through Nietzsche's work, and it's one I think that needs to be resolved. I should say that it's clearly not the centerpiece of Nietzsche's philosophy, although it recurs in many different works, and I think too many commentators recently have taken this as being the most important thing that Nietzsche had to say. In particular, some of the postmodernists in France, especially, have taken Nietzsche's view that there is no truth and his emphasis on rhetoric to say that Nietzsche, in fact, doesn't make any assertions, that philosophy itself should be reduced to literature, that, in fact, philosophy really doesn't have much to say. Even science is just another kind of literary discourse.

Nietzsche, I think, would have rejected such views utterly out of hand. He would have considered them nonsense and worse. He would have considered them absolutely antithetical to being everything that someone who is interested in Wissenschaft should be. Nevertheless, let us talk about this paradox, this apparent contradiction, because then, I think, we are going to get a lot clearer about some of the things Nietzsche says of the much more polemical and practical nature later on. First of all, as always, there is a kind of ad hominem argument. I ended the last lecture by suggesting one version of it, and this is a sense in which Nietzsche turns against science, in which he asks why science, or, more specifically, why scholars in general, "scholarly oxen," as he calls them at one point, are so devoted to the truth. The question is, Why is truth important?

This seems like a nonsense question for someone who is already devoted to the truth. But, of course, if you are devoted to the truth, one of the questions that has to come up is the question, Why are we interested in truth? And Nietzsche asks at one point, very polemically, Why must we have truth at any cost? And, of course if you think about it, it's often come at a great cost. Individual lives have been ruined. Scientists back in the sixteenth and seventeenth centuries were burned at the stake for their beliefs, or they lost their status, or they were excommunicated. People have often been in a position of virtually upsetting an entire civilization with their ideas. Freud comes to mind as an obvious example. So there is a sense in which the costs of truth are tremendous. And what Nietzsche wants to ask is, Why are we willing to pay them?

As always, it's a question about motivation and, to sort of set up the general scheme of the entire lecture, it's going to be that the search for truth can't be viewed as an isolated phenomenon but, rather, the search for truth is, like everything else, part of life and has to be understood on more general principles that have to do with how we live our life in general. Some obvious examples: Sometimes the search for truth is really a search for a certain kind of status. The philosopher who comes up with the right theory; the scientist who comes up with the best hypothesis—they have a certain kind of status in their profession. So, one can say, why are they after the truth? Well, it may be that they are interested in the problem, but, first and foremost, they are motivated by the need to have status. Watson, in his description of his work with Crick on the analysis of DNA, is quite straightforward about the fact that what moved them was, more than any thing else, their competition with their fellow scientists to discover the structure first.

Another explanation is that the truth, in fact, is not an end in itself, not something pursued for its own sake, but truth is something that is pursued for other goals. The most notable example is the well-known phrase; "The truth shall make you free." That fact is inscribed on one of the Texas University buildings. It's something that we often pass, as philosophers, with a mixture of pride and curiosity. But the idea that the truth will make you free, of course, is to say precisely: the truth itself is not the end; truth is a means. Truth leads to freedom. Also, the idea of truth lends itself to a kind of sense of the absolute. If you have the truth—and you get this picture of the truth as rock hard and immovable, and, of course, since ancient times, often the truth, reality, is also eternal—from that standpoint, you are in a powerful position.

And, of course, as so often in Nietzsche, the search for truth is going to get analyzed in terms of the search for power. Looking for truth is itself an honorable, praiseworthy, high-status enterprise, and, as well, having the truth, claiming to have the truth, puts you in a privileged position. Why are people so adamant about the truth? They are adamant about the truth because it makes them in some way important. Nevertheless, Nietzsche's arguments about truth, insofor as he does give us arguments, suggest something else as well. Take, for example, the idea that there is no truth; there are only interpretations. Well, one way to think about that is that there is no way of getting to the bottom of things.

Take, for example, a text, and let's take the obvious, most important example for many of us, the Bible. You take a text, and you have to right away admit the obvious. A former governor of Texas said something like, in an argument over bilingual education, "If English was good enough for Jesus, it's good enough for us." But, of course, it's not hard to realize that the Bible that we read is a translation. More accurately, it's a translation of a translation of a translation of a translation, and, as everyone knows who's ever translated anything, there are all sorts of questions of interpretation that enter in at each step. It's not just presenting the original text, but it's already presenting the original text transformed, and, one might argue, distorted.

In the case of the Bible, of course we know it's not just a matter of having an original text because it's a text that was cobbled together from many different texts, and those different texts themselves were interpretations of events, interpretations of myths and stories, interpretations for which there could be no original evidence, in many cases. So what we are talking about, if we are talking about the Bible as a text, it's not really a text at all. Rather, it is a series of interpretations, one on top of the other, going back to a set of facts that are themselves indeterminable. So to say that there is no truth, there are only interpretations, is to say that everything, not just texts but our own experience, is an interpretation based on other interpretations based on other interpretations.

For example, take any common experience—the experience, for example, of wearing a wristwatch. Well, why do I think it's a wristwatch? Well, because I have been brought up in this culture, and I have been taught that that's what this thing is, and I know quite a bit about what it does, if not anything about how it does it. What's more, the whole notion of a wristwatch is built not just into the culture, but there is a sense in which it requires the use of language. I can imagine someone from a very different kind of culture looking at it and thinking of it as nothing but a bracelet, an ornament of some sort, or perhaps as a rather grotesque aberration of my skin on my wrist.

There's a sense in which to understand anything is to interpret it, and, if you want to work your way back to the original facts on which it's based, Nietzsche will tell us, there are no such facts. There is no original text; it's all experience, and experience is always an interpretation of something else. There is a sense in which, when Nietzsche talks about there being no truth, only appearances, that, too, presents us with a kind of paradox. For example, there is a sense in which to talk about appearances is automatically to talk about the appearance of something. If I see an appearance of Kathy, the presumption is that Kathy is there, or, if not, the appearance resembles Kathy; perhaps I'm hallucinating. But it refers to Kathy; there has got to be a Kathy for there to be an appearance of Kathy.

Well, there's a sense in which appearances, then, are dependent. Appearances depend on there being something of which there are appearances. But now we ask the question, How do you ever get behind the appearances? Now, this, of course, is an old philosophical question. It's perhaps most famous in modern philosophy through someone like Descartes, who asked this kind of skeptical question, How do I know that my experiences aren't fooling me? Or, the kind of human skepticism, in a much more radical way: How do I know my experiences refer to anything at all? Of course, it goes back to the early Greeks because they were skeptics, too, and they asked questions of a similar sort. You find them even in Plato.

But the idea here is that, in talking about appearances, in talking about the world as it is in itself, what we always end up talking about is a gap between the experience, the appearances, on the one hand, and what they are appearances or experiences of on the other. Kant, perhaps, makes it most explicit when he talks about the world of our experience as distinguished from the world in itself—the world as it might be apart from our experiences. But there is always this problem, which every philosopher has had to face: How can you even assert such a thing, if there is no way of getting behind the experience, of going behind the appearances and seeing reality itself?

Some philosophers have concluded from this that it's nonsense to talk about this at all. Other philosophers have tried many different tricks of logic, of science, to try to show how we can defend what we believe, what we experience, on the basis of some sort of proof, on the basis of some sort of inference. But, however you do this, you are always left with a deep puzzle: How can you even talk about experiences as opposed to reality if you can never compare the experiences and reality to see if they match up?

Nietzsche struggles with this question virtually all of his career, and I think the way to understand many of his more enigmatic statements about truth, such things as "there is no truth," is to understand that all are stages in his grappling with this basic paradox. Nietzsche's ultimate resolution is to see his way through the paradox and—as he puts it in one of his more striking aphorisms, actually a six-part aphorism—he says, in the conclusion, let's get rid of the real world, and, with the real world, the apparent world disappears, too. In other words, to take Kant and Hegel at, in one sense, their most generous, one might say that what they discovered and what Nietzsche is now discovering for himself is that the very distinctions that philosophers have made since ancient times, since Parmenides, between reality on the one hand and appearance on the other, is a bogus distinction. There is only the world of our experience to talk about; anything else just doesn't make any sense.

But, now, what do we say about the world of our experience? Does it consist of facts; does it consist of truths? And let's be very clear that what Nietzsche is doing is emphatically not denying that some claims are more warranted than others, that we can't say anything truthful about ourselves or about the world. That is just plain wrong because Nietzsche is, among all philosophers, together with Socrates, one of the ones who is most adamant about seeing, in some sense, the truth, but the truth has to be understood in terms of interpretations, in terms of experiences.

So let's address the entire question from a different angle. There is a sense that comes out clearly in Kant of the world in itself, the world as God might perceive it, and Kant himself says that this is, for us, a notion bordering on nonsense because the truth is we have no conception whatsoever, we can't have a conception, of what such a world in itself might be. For Nietzsche, there is no such world in itself, but, more importantly, there is no God's-eye view—no way—

not just because there is no God, but because, even if there were a God, as I said in a very early lecture, even if there were a God, He would still have to see the world from a perspective, even though it's a God's perspective.

The truth is, we always see the world from a perspective, and I indicated in the last lecture that, for example, we can look at the world—a flower growing on a table—from a scientific perspective, or we can look at it from an aesthetic perspective. We can look at certain questions, for example, the miracles described in the Old and New Testaments. We can look at those as religious truths, or we can look at them as scientific questions. How could this have happened? How can this be explained? We can, in our lives, take a view of ourselves as a parent, ourselves as a teacher, ourselves as still a child, ourselves as citizens, ourselves as citizens of the world. Now, with each shift in perspective, what we are doing is, in a way, changing the truths. That's not to say that there is no truth.

But now what we have started to do is we have started to relativize truth, and I want to be very careful here not to relativize in a vicious way but simply to say, at this point, that what we are doing is appreciating that what might be a truth from one point of view, say, a religious point of view, might not be a truth from, say, a scientific point of view. The debate between creationists and evolutionists, for example—I think one way of resolving that dispute, which even the Pope himself has accepted, is that there is a religious point of view of the matter and there is a scientific point of view of the matter, and the one doesn't exclude the other; they are simply different perspectives, different ways of accounting for and appreciating the same set of phenomena.

This idea in Nietzsche, which, especially in his experimental period when he is writing *Human, All Too Human*; *Daybreak*; and *Gay Science*, is conceived of in terms of a view that is now called "perspectivsm." Nietzsche didn't label his views for the most part, but this one is pretty close to what he himself regarded as his. Perspectivism is the view that there are lots of different viewpoints we can take on things, and, what's more, it's not as if as the word "perspective," which is visual metaphor, would suggest that there is something of which these are different perspectives. One might say, rather unhelpfully, that it's life or it's the world, the world of experience.

©1999 The Teaching Company.

But, ultimately, what you want to say is, simply, this is the perspective, this is the context, this is the truth that emerges from that perspective, and, of course, from within a perspective, one can argue quite vigorously about what evidence there is, about what follows from the evidence, about what hypothesis is more plausible than another hypothesis, or, moving from science to aesthetics, what is a more beautiful or the most beautiful way of looking at something. So it's not as if perspectivism rules out the question of argument, debate, or the search for truth, but, rather, it says, this is always to be conceived of as contextualized.

Now, perspectivism itself is a fascinating theory. In fact, perhaps the most exciting example of it, which we are going to talk about at great length in several coming lectures, is the possibility of different moral perspectives, and, of course, this goes back to when I began this lecture with the idea that there is always a motive for seeking the truth. The idea of different moral perspectives might again be used to raise the question, Why do scientists, philosophers, and scholars devote themselves to the search for truth, often eliminating many of the other happinesses of normal human life—social life, family? The answer, in part, might be because of personal status, the search for freedom, the need for power. But Nietzsche's perfectly willing to allow that there is something like a little automatic mechanism that gets scholars and scientists going looking for the truth.

Nevertheless, this is something that has to be explained in terms of their personalities, in terms of the context, in terms of the kind of encouragement they get from their culture. In general, science is a definitive perspective, but so are many other things, and, in morality in particular, we are going to see two very different perspectives. In fact, there will be many more. But the two very different perspectives are the ones that Nietzsche calls "master and slave morality." These are not just simply two different cultural artifacts. They are not simply two different ways of looking at morality, but they're two very different perspectives on the world, and here in particular something very important comes through—that talking about different perspectives is not to say that any perspective is on a par or just as good as any other perspective, and Nietzsche is going to be very cautious here. On the one hand, he wants to be clear that, look, people do hold the one perspective and they hold the other perspective and that's their perspective, but, at the same time, there is no question, when reading Nietzsche on morality, that he considers the master perspective the better one and for lots of reasons, which we will go into in some detail.

In general, this notion of perspectivism, as I suggested in the second lecture, has to be distinguished, at least from a vicious sense, of relativism, relativism that says every view is as good as any other. Not true. But I think it can be allied to relativism in what I call the innocent and almost obvious sense, and that is that different truths, different hypotheses, different suggestions of all different sorts are necessarily in a context and that means in a perspective. Now, what does a philosopher do? What a philosopher should do is essentially adopt as many perspectives as possible, and, this, I think, is the philosophical explanation behind many of Nietzsche's stylistic devices, particularly the device of the aphorism.

As Kathy indicated in her discussion, there are may different perspectives one can take on a given aphorism, and, also, within a book, often within the same section, Nietzsche will give a number of aphorisms on more or less the same topic, sometimes taking seemingly opposed points of view, which has led many philosophers to accuse him of inconsistency and to Karl Jaspers, who is one of Nietzsche's earlier admirers, saying that Nietzsche never finds any claim without looking for its contradiction. That's a bit excessive, but I think there is a very important point that lies behind it, and, that is, with Nietzsche it is always a matter of not simply taking one position and digging in. Philosophers make their whole career taking a position and digging it in, protecting it against all comers, but philosophy is shifting positions.

I often say to my students, as a very important exercise, particularly for those who are particularly dogmatic about one position or another, that I want them to write me a short paper in which they take the opposed position. If they are Christian fundamentalists, I want them to write a paper against Christian fundamentalism. If they are atheists, I want them to write a paper in defense of atheism. In general, I think it's very important to keep shifting perspectives, and according to Nietzsche, what the philosopher is supposed to do as part of his experimentalism is to keep shifting views so that you appreciate how these different views first of all operate in their own terms but then, more generally, understand how these different perspectives operate together.

Where is the truth? Well, I talked about the truth within a perspective, particularly, of course, if we are talking about a scientific perspective, but there is also a larger truth, what Hegel, for example, called philosophical truth. It's not something that lies behind the appearances; it's not something that only God can know, but, rather, philosophical truth is getting this sense, this very large and ever-increasing sense, of how these different perspectives, how these different ways of looking at things, all tie together.

Now, that's not the end of the story. One part of the story, of course, is to talk about multiple perspectives, or to talk about what William James refers to as pluralism—to allow for the problematic possibility, for many people, that you must entertain or be able to entertain different viewpoints and different truths, perhaps at the same time. Emerson famously said that consistency is the hobgoblin of little minds. Nietzsche, of course, admired Emerson quite greatly, and I can imagine that this is one way of characterizing Nietzsche's philosophy, too.

Now, by inconsistency, he doesn't mean the sort of flat, logical contradiction that philosophers are appalled by, but, rather, he is talking about different perspectives. Why can't you be a scientist and evolutionist and a creationist at the same time? Why can't you be a chemist who understands the chemistry of oil paint and at the same time appreciates the beauty of a particular painting? There is no reason, but philosophical sophistication and the philosophical skill that we should be cultivating in ourselves is precisely this ability to hold these different perspectives in mind at the same time.

But something more. Nietzsche, as we have suggested several times now, is a quasi follower of Darwin, and Nietzsche being Nietzsche, often emphasizes his disagreements more than he underscores his agreements. But his agreements with Darwin, in fact, are multiple and profound. One, of course, is that Darwin says, in effect, that we are animals and we should be understood in terms of the general trend of evolution. Nietzsche thoroughly agrees with this. But he agrees with Darwin in another sense, too, and although he doesn't talk much about natural selection—in fact, he has some arguments against it—one can see Nietzsche's view of truth very much in terms of something like Darwinian notions of fitness.

Today this would be called by some philosophers "pragmatic theory of truth." The name comes from James and Dewey, but I think it really fits Nietzsche as well and has, as it does explicitly in James and Dewey, Darwinian roots. I want you to imagine how it comes about that people have certain kinds of beliefs. And here let's not talk about very particular beliefs, like coconuts grow on palm trees, but let's talk about very general beliefs, in fact, beliefs that are so general that they have been talked about by many modern philosophers as the presuppositions or the foundations of all knowledge. David Hume, for example, talks, for one, about the importance of induction and the idea that the future will resemble the past, and that's how we learn. He is a devout empiricist: we learn on the basis of experience, and we learn not just particular things, but we also learn, in some sense, the most basic things.

Hume's skepticism is very much caught up in the question, How do you defend these most basic principles? How do you defend the idea of induction? Kant comes along and answers Hume's question. Kant comes along and says, basically, that induction really amounts to one of the rules according to which the human mind operates: If something happens, then it is more likely to happen again. In general, the future will be like the past. It is built right into our minds. Well, Nietzsche is not going to stop it there. As always, Nietzsche wants to push the question, How did that belief get there— why is it built into the human mind? And a Darwinian answer makes perfectly good sense.

Suppose you imagine a species of creatures who have built into their brains the idea that the future will be unlike the past so that, if you see lightning strike a tall tree, you rush under the tree during the next storm, expecting that lightning will never strike twice in the same place, or, having struck a tall tree this time, lightning will strike somewhere else next time. The odds are that such a species would be short-lived. On the other hand, a species that developed an inductive mind, that learned from experience, is much more likely to survive and flourish.

So, when Nietzsche asks, What are our truths? —In fact, taking up from Kant even our synthetic *a priori* truths, those basic foundational truths—he says, they are the indispensable errors of mankind. They are the truths without which we would not as a species survive, but if what you are asking is, "Does this correspond to some real world apart from experience?" the answer is, "That's a nonsensical question."

Lecture Twelve

"Become Who You Are"—
Freedom, Fate, and Free Will

Scope:

"Freedom" was the watchword of the eighteenth and nineteenth centuries, but what it meant was a matter of great controversy. In politics, freedom was interpreted (e.g., by Enlightenment "liberals") mainly in terms of *laissez-faire*, "leave us alone." By contrast, many thinkers followed a less negative sense of freedom in terms of the freedom to participate, to elevate oneself in society, to create. Nietzsche's political views cannot be easily stated or separated from the times in which he formulated them: the age of Bismarck, militant German unification under Prussia, German chauvinism, the strong socialist and democratic currents sweeping through Europe, the influence of Darwin. Against German chauvinism, the statism and military Reich of Bismarck, Nietzsche declared himself "a good European." Insofar as Nietzsche had a political philosophy, it was centered on the freedom to create. Nietzsche is well known for his individualism, his notorious views on "the great man." But there was, and is, another dimension to freedom, a metaphysical dimension, which has to do with whether or not an individual can ever be free at all, that is free from his or her heredity, upbringing, and circumstances. Nietzsche, who is often linked to the freedom-loving "existentialists," nevertheless denies any such freedom.

Outline

I. Nietzsche is often presented as a champion of freedom, as one of the existentialists. This is in some senses true, in other senses false.

    A. Nietzsche rejects the "negative" political view of freedom (*laissez-faire*), which he views with alarm as mere lack of discipline and as license.

        1. More popular in Germany was a positive view of freedom, the freedom to do or be something else.

        2. This amounts to freedom within limits.

    B. Nietzsche rejects democracy and with it the freedom for all to participate in the determination of values.

1. Only the rare few are in a position to create values or determine the course of history.
2. Nietzsche shares this anti-democratic view with Socrates, but he does not endorse the idea of "Philosopher-Kings."

C. What Nietzsche clearly believed in was the freedom to create.
   1. Nietzsche did not believe that the state was in any position to spur or encourage creativity.
   2. He did not think that one was free to become creative if one was not already born with talent.

II. Nietzsche is well-known for his individualism.

A. Individualism is a "modern" creation.
   1. It originated in the twelfth century with the invention of "courtly love."
   2. The Renaissance promoted individualism after it rediscovered the ancients.

B. We should distinguish between the individual's ability to create and to choose alternative actions.
   1. Kierkegaard emphasizes the choice.
   2. Sartre emphasizes the individual's absolute freedom to choose. We are responsible for who we are and what we do.

C. For Nietzsche, there are constraints on the determinants of our behavior.
   1. The individual is not free to choose whatever he or she will do.
   2. In this sense, Nietzsche is *not* like the existentialists, e.g., Jean-Paul Sartre.
   3. Nietzsche is a biological determinist. He thinks that what we are, we are for the most part from birth.
   4. What he does allow is that we are free to "become who we are" (a phrase from the Greek poet Pindar). We can and should realize our natural talents and character.
   5. In this view of character, he follows Schopenhauer, who thought that every person was unique. Nietzsche, unlike Schopenhauer, really does see us as individuals, not as manifestations of one Will.

6. Nietzsche asks: Do we *decide* to behave in certain ways? For him, the "self" is naturalistic and empirical.

III. Nietzsche rejects the idea of the Will, but he also rejects the idea of free will. Free will presupposes a notion of the subject or self that is a metaphysical fiction.

  A. Nietzsche's view of the self is purely naturalistic and empirical.

  B. The notion of agency is therefore a problem for him.

  1. How much do we actually choose to do, and how much is simply an expression of our natures?

  2. How do we know that we are the agents of our own action?

IV. Nietzsche, like the early Greeks and unlike most moderns, believes in fate.

  A. He thinks that we each have a destiny, based on our given natures.

  B. This is why he defends *amor fati*, "the love of fate." It harks back to his earlier views on tragedy and accepting our life, even in the midst of suffering, loving it. In short, the individual must take responsibility for who he/she is.

Essential Reading:

Twilight of the Idols, "Four Great Errors," and "What We Owe to the Ancients."

Supplemental Reading:

T. Strong, "Nietzsche's Political Misappropriation" in Richard Schacht, ed., *Nietzsche: Selections*; *Genealogy, Morality*, pp. 119–150.

————, "Nietzsche and Politics" in Robert C. Solomon, ed., *Nietzsche*, pp. 258–293.

Questions to Consider:

1. What is an individual, according to Nietzsche? How does this jibe with our more ordinary sense of what it is to be an individual?

2. Do you believe in fate? Why does Nietzsche? What does it mean to believe in fate?

Lecture Twelve—Transcript

"Become Who You Are"—
Freedom, Fate, and Free Will

When I started teaching philosophy many years ago, I was asked by my then department if I would teach a course called "Hegel, Nietzsche, and Existentialism." It was a course created by the eminent Nietzsche scholar Walter Kaufmann, and the title itself gives rise to a very interesting question. Nietzsche is often considered as one of the existentialists—not Nietzsche *and* existentialism at all—and the question about whether he should be so classified is a very interesting and complicated one. I love both Nietzsche and the existentialists, thinking of existentialism as that movement of eccentrics from the mid-nineteenth century with the religious thinker Kierkegaard and culminating in the philosophy of the French philosopher Jean Paul-Sartre.

The watchword of existentialism is freedom, and so, in many ways, the question about whether Nietzsche is or is not an existentialist comes down to the question of, Does Nietzsche agree with the existentialists on the importance and centrality and nature of freedom? I think the answer, which, of course, will satisfy no one, is both yes and no. Freedom is a word that, of course, has a very long philosophical and theological history, but sticking to modern times, freedom was, in one sense, the watchword of the Enlightenment, and, in many ways, freedom was represented by the very liberal stance, which said, in French, *laissez-faire*, or "leave us alone." It's a conception of freedom that is largely negative. In other words, we should be left apart from government interference, interference by the majority, interference from whatever moral forces or institutions might want to step in our territory.

But, in Germany, in particular, that notion of freedom was not thought well of because it represented a kind of negative freedom. It said, here's what shouldn't happen to us, but it didn't say anything much about what we should do. So, in Germany, in particular, the notion of freedom that developed was a sense of positive freedom, a sense of freedom not from constraints and interference, but freedom—freedom to participate, freedom to be a part of something, freedom to educate oneself, freedom to have a career. And so the freedom that develops in Germany, unlike, for example, the freedom that was dominant in much of the rhetoric in England and France, was a freedom that wasn't simply a matter of individual choice and wasn't simply a matter of freedom from interference, but, rather, it had to do with the freedom to do or to be something else.

In Nietzsche, in particular, insofar as the word "freedom" means anything like what the other philosophers meant by it, freedom is going to be the freedom to be or rather to become who one is. Now, Nietzsche rejects negative freedom on many grounds. For one thing, he rejects democracy in general. He rejects it because he thinks mere choice, majority choice, or the choice of people in general by any scheme who are uneducated, who are inexperienced in the ways of government or inexperienced in the culture, should not count for very much. Their interests should be taken into account, of course. Their needs must be taken into account. Nevertheless, there is a sense in which freedom does not have anything like the meaning that we in America, for example, so often give to it in which freedom and democracy are so closely linked.

In general, the idea of freedom as simply freedom from constraint is something that Nietzsche would look down upon as being a kind of a fantasy, and, in fact, it's the fantasy, as we will see, of so many other things of the oppressed. The truth is, if you simply give someone, let's say, a paintbrush and a canvas and you say, "Do whatever you want," what you are probably going to get is junk, and the reason for this is that great art and great things in general are not expressions of freedom from all constraint but quite the contrary. The great poet Goethe, whom Nietzsche often refers to, had an expression that he shared with many of his colleagues, and the expression was "freedom within limits."

It's the limits that define greatness. If you think of that form of Japanese painting, for example, where you get just one brush stroke—once you have lifted the brush from the paper you are done—that is a challenge, and some great creativity comes out of it. Or—to stick with the Japanese for a second—if you compose a poem in Haiku, you get a fixed number of syllables, no more and no less, and the talent, the creativity, is seeing what you can do within that very constrained medium. So it is with human life. We are constrained by many things. We are constrained by our culture, by our tradition, by our biology, by the circumstances of history, and although we can struggle against them and, in some sense, even reject them, nevertheless, they are always there as constraints on our behavior, and freedom, if it is to mean anything at all, has to be freedom within those limitations.

Freedom for Nietzsche, I think, could be summarized in one phrase, and it by far is most important to him. As we have said in earlier lectures, Nietzsche is not particularly political, although he does have some nasty things to say about democracy and about socialism and about some other social movements. But, in fact, what Nietzsche is concerned about is the individual and, in particular, creativity. The phrase I think that captures Nietzsche's view of freedom is "the freedom to create," and the ultimate ideal of a culture, of a politics, is, in addition to doing the sorts of routine things that politics has to do, more than anything else, to cultivate citizens who can create, people who can move forward the culture, people who can express what that culture is, and, of course, people who can think for themselves and experiment, as Nietzsche tries to do, in new ways.

I say Nietzsche is an individualist, but I want to be very careful with that, too, because there is a sense in which the individual is a very bourgeois notion. There is a sense in which individualism is a modern creation, and historians, in fact, have pinpointed it very carefully. The notion of the individual comes prominent basically in the twelfth century. Now, the twelfth century is interesting for all sorts of reasons. The twelfth century is when the Crusades were going on; the twelfth century is when feudalism was breaking down; the twelfth century is when traditional, marital, and social arrangements were falling apart; the twelfth century is when love was invented in its courtly style in southern France by the troubadours. In the twelfth century, because of the breakdown of the social fabric, because of the emphasis on what we now would refer to as romantic love, because of the need for people to find their own way in the world, the concept of the individual became increasingly important.

With the Renaissance, in particular, there was a rediscovery of the ancients, who, by the way, were not individualists but nevertheless had a sense of individualism that was nevertheless more robust than, for example, what we had inherited from the medieval traditions. In the eighteenth century, in the nineteenth century, both the Enlightenment and Romanticism emphasized individualism to a very large degree—the Enlightenment because the individual was the unit of reason, the unit of society, and it was a common Enlightenment view that a society was nothing but the cooperation and the getting together of individuals. In fact, even the contracts, which they would form according to which they would be members of society, had the implication, as was evidenced in the French Revolution, that, if they didn't like the terms of the contract, or if the contract was breached, they could turn away and remain individuals.

In Romanticism, the picture is a bit more complicated. On the one hand, Romanticism specializes in this kind of cosmic view, the sort of thing I described in the Friedrich painting of the cloudy landscape or the Wagner overture in which we get these swelling senses of the universe, Schopenhauer's will. But at the same time, the individual is a very important piece of the picture. What's interesting of course, from a historical point of view, is how, with this emphasis on the cosmic and the universal, or, in the Enlightenment case, on universal reason, and, on the other hand, the individual as the emphasis, what gets left out in the middle is, to a large extent, the family, community, politics.

Alisdair MacIntyre says in one of his books that, in reading the eighteenth-century philosophers, the one conclusion he is forced to is that none of them had families, but, of course, the same would be true of Nietzsche. Nietzsche talks very much about the individual, even the lone individual, but doesn't talk that much about society, which he sometimes refers to as the herd, and, insofar as he talks about the cosmos, it's usually in a rather artful, not very scientific, and certainly not metaphysical, way.

What's important for Nietzsche is the individual and the individual's ability to create, but this has to be distinguished from what we might call the individual's ability to choose, and there's a very central core of Nietzsche's philosophy, which is, in this sense, very unlike the existentialists. If you look at someone like Kierkegaard, the most important thing is to choose. Kierkegaard outlines for us a number of possible ways of existence, what we would call lifestyles. He says, for example, one could be an artist or a hedonist; one could be a very moral person; one could be a religious devotee as he was, but this can't be defended on rational grounds, and, what's more, there are no ultimate reasons why an individual should choose one mode rather than another. Rather, the important thing is the choice itself.

So one chooses to be a Christian as he did, and what that means is that one—kind of in a vacuum of sorts—commits oneself to this alternative and, in so doing, pushes aside the others. Or, in Jean-Paul Sartre this century—what we find in Sartre is a powerful metaphysical thesis, a sort of story about the nature of human existence in which the absolute freedom, his phrase "the absolute freedom of the individual to choose" is always with us, and Sartre has a very harsh notion of freedom. We are responsible because we have chosen everything. We are responsible for what we do even if it doesn't seem as if we have chosen it—as if we just happened upon it; we are nevertheless responsible. We could have somehow resisted. We are responsible for who we are. This is something that we become through our various choices, and we are responsible for the state of society.

If there is still poverty, then we are responsible for it because we haven't chosen to do enough, and, what's more, we are responsible for humanity and what human being means because if I decide to be selfish, possibly with the rationalization, "Well, everyone is selfish," what I am doing is not jut making a decision for myself, but I am implicitly stating, "Here is what it means to be human," and I am, in effect, encouraging other people to make the same kind of decision, in which case human nature will be selfish because that's what we have decided.

Now, all this is emphatically un-Nietzschian. For Nietzsche, the whole question of choice is something that's thrown into a radical kind of questioning. He is not like Sartre; he is not like Kierkegaard, although he resembles them pretty well in other aspects, but, unlike them, he says there are always not only constraints on our behavior, but there are determinants of our behavior, something which Sartre quite exclusively denies. We make choices, for Sartre, again, in a kind of vacuum in which causal accounts, causal explanations about neurology, about our upbringing, our psychology, about human nature—all of this is put in suspension as we make the choice. For Nietzsche, that's impossible.

One might say that Nietzsche is a biological determinist. I don't want to take this too strictly, but what it means is in line with many other things we have said now about Nietzsche's emphasis on naturalism, about his emphasis on drives and instincts, many of which come down to us from our heritage rather than being things that we learn through our culture. There is a sense in which Nietzsche wants to say that what appear to be choices aren't really choices at all. Rather, it's a kind of destiny, and this can all sound very mysterious, and I will try to make it a little bit more mysterious at the end of the lecture.

But I think the right way to think about it is in terms of a phrase that he picks up from the Greek poet Pindar. We have mentioned it before. It's a very simple phrase. It says, "Become who you are." Well, that's a fascinating notion! It's not "who you are," the kind of unhelpful advice that teenagers get from their parents when they are going out on a date and they are told, "Just be yourself, dear." They get a rightful look of, "What??" On the other hand, there is a sense in which to say "be who you are" implies a kind of stasis, something that doesn't change. For Nietzsche, this sort of line between freedom and un-freedom, between choice and lack of choice, here gets very blurry because what he wants to say is that we are all born with certain sorts of abilities, talents, potentials—some more, some less— but virtually none of us is simply raised in such a way or thrown in such circumstances that these simply emerge.

Rather, it's the case that cultivating who one is a lifelong effort, that, when he says in *The Birth of Tragedy* life is to be justified only as an aesthetic phenomenon and the theme that sort of goes through is "live your life as a work of art," what's implied there is something very much like Goethe's notion of freedom within limitation, that the creativity of the individual is, to a large extent, creating oneself but not on a blank canvas with a set of oil paints and the instructions "anything goes," certainly a very popular American belief, something that one can read rather easily in the philosophy of Sartre. Quite to the contrary, it's a very limited canvas, and it's a very limited palate, and what one can paint is restricted as, for example, one of those Japanese paintings where you only get one line, that line being your life.

There is a sense in which, when Nietzsche says, following Pindar, "Become who you are," what he is talking about is something that is very ancient in a way. It's a thesis that was defended by Aristotle and that is defended often today under the name of self-realization. Or, it's even self-fulfillment, although that smacks too much of just trying to be happy. The idea of self-realization is that you are born into a certain pattern, into a family, into a social class, into a culture, into a tradition, and all that says a great deal about who you could be. And although Nietzsche clearly adopts this kind of lion-like posture of saying "no" of roaring against the tradition, and although he praises the creativity of a child, the simple fact of the matter is children are born in a vacuum.

Children are not born into families; children are born learning one language or two languages rather than the others; children are born into a culture, into a tradition. They are raised in certain ways and, depending on which of the psychoanalysts you believe, by the time you are two or four or seven or at least thirteen, you pretty much are the person you are. Or, rather, you have already shown the basic shape of the person you can become.

I remember several years ago—I won't tell you how many—I went to my high school reunion. It was a fascinating endeavor, something I recommend to everyone. Of course, when I talk to my college students about it, they can't think of anything less interesting. But, believe me, when you get fifteen to twenty years out of high school and go back and meet your old classmates, most of whom you haven't seen or heard from in all that time, something becomes transparently obvious and that is, with only a few exceptions, that they still are the person they were in high school. They have grown in a number of different dimensions, but, nevertheless, they're the same person.

In an obvious sort of analogy, you see a smooth twiglet in the ground that is sprouting from, say, an acorn, and if you came back fifty years later, it might be a mighty oak tree. But what would be interesting would be that the basic shape of the oak tree was evident even in the little twiglet, that it grows, it goes through enormous changes, but what it changes into is a fulfillment, a realization, of itself. Now, in the oak tree case, it's pretty clear that the notion of choice doesn't make any sense at all. In the human case, Sartre would say, the choice is really everything, whatever the circumstances, whatever the shape you were given as a child. He says this against Freud, for example: it is your responsibility what you become.

Not so for Nietzsche. For Nietzsche, there are many choices along the way, but the choices are all already along this dimension in accordance with this shape. So, for example, as a teenager we all have the possibility, and, unfortunately, the likelihood, of making a number of ruinous choices, choices that will, in effect, block our development and our self–realization. Of course, we also have choices the other side of those, choices that, although we may not realize it until later, are choices that will augment, enhance, help us along in that road to self-realization. And often we don't know what they are. Again, Nietzsche often says one has to trust one's instincts, that when one acts on the basis of what we would call impulse, on the basis of gut feelings, one is very often much more in tune with the person you are or could become than when you reason.

In fact, reason once again is a certain kind of problem because, with reason, what we are often doing is accepting the wisdom of the culture around us, which may or may not be suited for us, and, if what we can be is creative individuals, then accepting what's already been given is going to be quite against our ultimate interests. This is a point again where Nietzsche follows and doesn't follow Schopenhauer. Schopenhauer talked about species in general as if they were the manifestation of a single idea. So there's an important sense in which one horse is like any other horse, in which one dog is like any other dog—with which I, of course, vehemently disagree—but, nevertheless, the idea is that, among the animals and the plants and in nature more generally, there is a sense in which an idea simply takes on different manifestations—slightly different shapes and forms—but, ultimately, it's the same idea.

With human beings, however, every person has his or her own idea. Now, we are not here talking about the kind of ideas you might have in your mind, but, rather, each one has their own particular destiny, their own particular character to fill out. And, for Schopenhauer, much of an understanding of human nature is to understand it on the basis of this kind of individuality, but, of course, this individuality is compromised by the fact that, within each of us, what drives us is ultimately this universal will, which pushes us to various desires and urges and various ultimately irrational directions.

Nietzsche, while accepting certain pieces of this picture, for example, the individualist aspect of it, nevertheless rejects others and, in particular, as we've already noted, he rejects Schopenhauer's notion of the universal will. There is a sense in which the will is in each one of us, but, even there, Nietzsche wants to raise some skeptical questions. Do we have a will in the sense that either Schopenhauer or, more rationalistically, Kant suggests? When we do things, do we decide to do them, or, rather, is in some sense the deed done through us? This raises a number of very complicated questions, all of which have to do with, first of all, the notion of free will as it has been defended in philosophy ever since Augustine and, secondly the notion of the self, which, of course, has always been one of the foci of philosophy, particularly since Socrates.

In Nietzsche, the idea of the self, like everything else, is naturalistic; it's empirical. Now, this is to be distinguished from all those people who would say the self is ultimately the soul, and, in that sense, it is in some sense part of the other world or some aspect of the divine that's somehow in us. For Nietzsche, you might say it is secular all the way through. The self, if it exists at all, is going to be another feature of us that biology and psychology can simply explain. And to say that the self is empirical is to disagree with Kant, who talked about the self in very grandiose terms, the self as transcendental, the agent behind all of our knowledge, or talking about the self as the self of freedom, who again, outside the causal or connections of the world, acts as if it can make free choices.

For Nietzsche, to reject the notion of the Will is to reject the notion of free will. To accept such a notion of self is to reject the idea that there is something in us, something different from our biological being, that can make choices, that can apply concepts, that can do all the things that these philosophers had suggested. In fact, agency itself becomes a problem for Nietzsche as it had been for Schopenhauer. Now, for Schopenhauer, the reason is fairly straightforward. Even though he talks about us as individuals, what ultimately drives us is not something that belongs to us individually at all but the will. For Nietzsche, it's somewhat a more subtle problem.

The more subtle problem is that talking about agency, talking about free will, talking about choice in a way, for example, that Kant does, presumes that there is a self in us that, even if it's not part of another world, nevertheless, is a very curious independent subject that has only outward ties to our bodies, to the world, to our actions. So I can decide to do this or to be this or to make this change in the world, but Nietzsche asks the question, What kind of a self is that? And here again, what we get from Nietzsche are very often some rather outlandish statements, but, understood in context, it's a thesis that is well worth considering.

Put it this way. What makes us think that we are the agents of our own actions? In particular, why, when it comes to thinking, are we so sure that we are thinkers? This goes back to one of the classic phrases in philosophy, when Descartes declares, "I think; therefore, I am," and, even in his own day, some of his competitors were arguing, "Well, okay, yeah, it may be your thinking, but why do you think you are?" Or, more to the point and more philosophically, "Why do you think you are thinking?" Why not say something like, "There are thoughts present" and leave open the question of who is doing the thinking? Or Nietzsche says, in one of his very best aphorisms—in fact, one that Freud picks out as an inspiration for much that he does— "A thought comes when it will, not when I will."

If you think about your thinking, what becomes obvious is that thoughts sort of pop in, and, even if you have been working on a problem, as a great many brilliant scientists and creators have shown, it's very likely that you will pop up at three o'clock in the morning and there is the idea, there is the solution. Or, as I stand here talking to you, there is a strange sense in which I am not choosing the words that are coming out of my mouth. I mean, there is a sense in which something is going on of a very elaborate nature, but if I think in terms of what am I willing as I do this talking, the answer is I don't know. It's as if the words are just coming out.

The picture that Nietzsche wants to give us is that we overemphasize agency, and, with it, we overemphasize freedom, and we emphasize choice, and, getting back to the larger picture about becoming who you are, the truth is that we have to go back to a much earlier notion, which, of course, is very large in the Greeks and is often vulgarized. But it's the notion of fate. Nietzsche has a phrase, *amor fati*, "the love of fate," and what he means by this, in part, is a kind of acceptance of life and your life in particular, an acceptance of who you are, what your limitations are. But not just that; it is also this sense of having a destiny, the sense that you can and will be something if you work really hard to cultivate it, so it's anything but a quietist philosophy. He rejects the notion of freedom in the existential sense. Nevertheless, he emphasizes what the existentialists all emphasize and that is the importance of individual existence and seeing to it that *you* take responsibility for who you are.

Timeline

1844 October 15..............Nietzsche is born in Röcken, Saxony (Prussia).

1849..............Nietzsche's father dies at the age of 36.

1858–69..............Nietzsche studies the classics and music.

1869..............Nietzsche meets and befriends the composer, Richard Wagner.

1869..............Nietzsche becomes a professor of classics (philology) at Basel, Switzerland.

1870..............Bismarck unifies Germany. The Franco-Prussian war. Nietzsche enlists as an orderly.

1872..............Nietzsche publishes *The Birth of Tragedy*, idolizing the Greeks and Wagner.

1873–74..............Nietzsche publishes three "Untimely Meditations," including an essay on the German pessimist Arthur Schopenhauer.

1876..............Nietzsche publishes an essay on Wagner, as the break is becoming evident between them. Intermittent depression begins.

1878–79..............Nietzsche publishes *Human, All Too Human* (his first book of aphorisms), quits his job at Basel, but stays in Switzerland.

1881..............Nietzsche publishes *Daybreak*.

1882..............Nietzsche has a short but intense love affair with Lou Salomé. He publishes *The Gay Science*. Depression intensifies.

1883–85 ....Nietzsche writes and publishes *Thus Spoke Zarathustra*. His sister Elizabeth marries a proto-Nazi. Nietzsche is appalled and breaks with her.

1886 ....Nietzsche publishes *Beyond Good and Evil* and expands his *Gay Science*.

1887 ....Nietzsche publishes *On the Genealogy of Morals*, briefly considers a larger work to be called *The Will to Power*.

1888 ....Nietzsche publishes *The Wagner Case*, *Twilight of the Idols*, *The Antichrist*, and a quasi-autobiography, *Ecce Homo*.

1889 January ....Nietzsche collapses in Turin. He is moved in with his mother. He is now terminally demented.

1893 ....Nietzsche's sister returns from a failed fascist experiment in South America and takes over her brother's literary estate.

1897 ....Nietzsche's mother dies.

1900 August 25 ....Nietzsche dies in Weimar.

1916 ....*Thus Spoke Zarathustra* becomes the most popular book in the German trenches of World War I. The book is denounced in England and elsewhere.

1933 ....Elizabeth invites the newly elected Hitler to visit the newly built Nietzsche archives.

| 1950 | .... German-born refugee Walter Kaufmann expunges Nietzsche's now notorious association with fascism and the Nazis. Serious American Nietzsche scholarship begins. |

Glossary

Ad hominem: an argument against the person, not the position.

Agape: Christian love, love without *eros*, "the love of humanity."

Apollonian: the rational individuating element in Greek thought.

Dionysian: the frenzied, irrational, holistic element in the Greek spirit.

Eros: erotic (sexual) love.

Eternal recurrence: the idea that time and lives will repeat themselves, over and over.

"God is dead": Nietzsche's summary (borrowed from Luther and Hegel) that summarizes the end of monotheistic structure of Western thought.

Immoralism: anti-moral, or, in Nietzsche, the rejection of rule-bound ethics.

Last man: the evolutionary potential for the ultimate, satisfied *bourgeois*, Zarathustra's nightmare.

Macht: power, but especially the power of self-discipline and personal strength.

Master morality: a value system in which one's own nobility plays the central role.

Philia: love as friendship.

Reich: political power, "realm."

Ressentiment: a reactive but ineffective emotion, rejecting another's success.

Slave morality: a value system in which one's relative impotence plays the central role.

Transvaluation: turning a value system upside down, so that what was good is now evil, what was bad is now good.

Übermensch: the "superman," an evolutionary possibility, Zarathustra's dream.

Will to power: the ultimate motivation of human (and much animal) behavior.

Biographical Notes

Aeschulus (525–456 B.C.E.). Greek playwright, author of *Seven against Thebes* and *Prometheus Bound*. One of Nietzsche's favorite tragedians.

Bismarck, Otto von (1815–1898). Prussian statesman, consolidated the German *Reich*, ruled Germany for most of Nietzsche's adult life.

Darwin, Charles (1809–1882). English naturalist, father of the theory of evolution, author *of Origin of Species* and *The Ascent of Man*.

Descartes, René (1596–1650). French philosopher, mathematician, scientist, rationalist, "we think therefore we am," the man who "tyrannized consciousness," according to Nietzsche.

Emerson, Ralph Waldo (1803–1882). American philosopher, essayist, "Self-Reliance," admired by Nietzsche.

Euripides (480–405 B.C.E.). Greek playwright, author of *The Bacchae* and *Medea*. Nietzsche's least favorite tragedian.

Goethe, J. W. (1749–1832). German poet, culture hero, author of *Faust*. Nietzsche's most often-cited example of "the higher man."

Hegel, G.W.F. (1770–1831). History-minded German philosopher, cosmic rationalist, author of *The Phenomenology of Spirit* (1807) with its "Master-Slave" dialectic.

Heraclitus (540–480 B.C.E.). Pre-Socratic Greek philosopher, Nietzsche's favorite Greek philosopher.

Kant, Immanuel (1724–1804). German philosopher, uncompromising rationalist, author of the three Critiques, the *Critique of Pure Reason* (1781), *the Critique of Practical Reason* (1788) and the *Critique of Judgment* (1790). Nietzsche's most frequent target among philosophers.

Kierkegaard, Søren (1813–1855). Danish religious philosopher and first "existentialist." Many important parallels with Nietzsche, despite their very different positions on the desirability of Christianity.

Luther, Martin (1483–1546). German theologian, reformer, major figure in Nietzsche's Lutheran background.

Marx, Karl (1818–1883). German philosopher and socialist, author (with F. Engels) of *The Communist Manifesto* (1848).

Mill, John Stuart (1807–1858). English philosopher, one of Nietzsche's favorite targets (though rarely by name).

Nietzsche, Elizabeth Förster- (1846–1935). Nietzsche's sister, literary executor and self-appointed public relations agent.

Nietzsche, Franziska (1826–1895). Nietzsche's mother, often his closest friend and his devoted nurse for most of his last decade.

Nietzsche, Karl Ludwig (1813–1849). Nietzsche's father, a Lutheran minister, who died when Nietzsche was only four.

Paul of Tarsus (?–68). An apostle and one of the founders of Christianity, who attracts Nietzsche's harshest accusations for his attitudes toward the human body, sex, marriage, and human justice.

Pindar (522–438 B.C.E.). Greek poet, from whom Nietzsche gets his phrase "Become who you are."

Plato (428–347 B.C.E.). Greek philosopher, student and follower of Socrates, author of many dialogues with Socrates as key character, uncompromising rationalist. He shares much of the blame with his teacher for the over-rationalization of life.

Ree, Paul (1849–1901). German philosopher, friend of Nietzsche, author of a book on the moral sentiments.

Salomé, Lou Andreas (1861–1937). German philosopher, writer, friend of Nietzsche, author of one of the first books on Nietzsche.

Schopenhauer, Arthur (1788–1860). German philosopher, profound pessimist, author of *World as Will and Idea* (1819). Nietzsche's first and most profound modern philosophical influence.

Socrates (470–399 B.C.E.). Greek philosopher, gadfly, perished (didn't publish), Nietzsche's favorite target, also in many ways his role model.

Sophocles (525–456 B.C.E.). Greek playwright, author of the Oedipus trilogy. One of Nietzsche's favorite tragedians.

Spinoza, Baruch (1632–1677). Dutch philosopher, pantheist, determinist, author of the *Ethics*. Nietzsche eventually comes to consider him a "predecessor."

Wagner, Richard (1813–1883). German composer, Nietzsche's one-time friend and hero, creator of *Tristan and Isolde*, *Lohengrin*, the *Ring* cycle, and *Parsifal*.

Zarathustra (Zoroaster) (628–551 B.C.E.). Persian prophet, founder of Zoroastrianism, employed by Nietzsche as the protagonist of *Thus Spoke Zarathustra*.

Bibliography

Nietzsche's Works: German Editions

Kritische Gesamtausgabe Werke. Edited by Giogio Colli and Mazzino Montinari. Berlin: De Gruyter, 1967 onwards. The new standard edition.

Werke in Drei Bänden. 3 vols. Edited by Karl Schlechta. 3rd edition. Munich: Carl Hansers, 1965. The old standard edition.

Nietzsche in English Translation

Nietzsche's individual works (in chronological order, original publication dates in parentheses):

The Birth of Tragedy (with *The Case of Wagner*). Translated by Walter Kaufmann. New York: Vintage, 1966. (1872)

Untimely Meditations. Translated by R. J. Hollingdale. Cambridge: Cambridge University Press, 1983. (1873–1874)

David Strauss, Confessor and Writer. (1873)

On the Advantage and Disadvantage of History for Life. Also translated by Peter Preuss. Indianapolis: Hackett, 1980. (1874)

Schopenhauer as Educator. (1874)

Richard Wagner in Bayreuth. (1876)

Human, All Too Human. Translated by R. J. Hollingdale. Cambridge: Cambridge University Press, 1986. (1878)

Human, All Too Human II. Translated by R. J. Hollingdale. Cambridge: Cambridge University Press, 1986. (1879)

Daybreak: Thoughts on the Prejudices of Morality. Translated by R. J. Hollingdale. Cambridge: Cambridge University Press, 1982. (1881)

The Gay Science. Translated by Walter Kaufmann. New York: Vintage, 1974. (1882)

Thus Spoke Zarathustra. Translated by Walter Kaufmann. In *The Portable Nietzsche*, edited by Walter Kaufmann. New York: Viking, 1954. (1883–1885)

Beyond Good and Evil. Translated by Walter Kaufmann. New York: Vintage, 1966. (1886)

On the Genealogy of Morals. Translated by Walter Kaufmann and R. J. Hollingdale. (Together with *Ecce Homo*, translated by Walter Kaufmann.) New York: Vintage, 1967. (1887)

The Case of Wagner (with *The Birth of Tragedy*). Translated by Walter Kaufmann. New York: Vintage, 1966. (1888)

Twilight of the Idols. Translated by Walter Kaufmann. In *The Portable Nietzsche*, edited by Walter Kaufmann. New York: Viking, 1954. (1889)

The Antichrist. Translated by Walter Kaufmann. In *The Portable Nietzsche*, edited by Walter Kaufmann. New York: Viking, 1954. (1895)

Nietzsche contra Wagner. Translated by Walter Kaufmann. In *The Portable Nietzsche*, edited by Walter Kaufmann. New York: Viking, 1954. (1895)

Ecce Homo. Translated by Walter Kaufmann. (With *On the Genealogy of Morals*, translated by Walter Kaufmann and R. J. Hollingdale). New York: Vintage, 1967. (1895)

Letters and Unpublished Works

Philosophy and Truth: Selections from Nietzsche's Notebooks of the Early 1870's. Edited and translated by Daniel Breazeale. Atlantic Highlands, New Jersey: Humanities Press, 1979.

Selected Letters of Friedrich Nietzsche. Edited and translated by Christopher Middleton. Indianapolis: Hackett Publ. Co., 1996.

The Will to Power. Translated by Walter Kaufmann and R. J. Hollingdale. New York: Vintage, 1967 (compiled from the *Nachlass*, originally edited by Elizabeth Förster-Nietzsche).

Collections of Nietzsche's Works

Basic Writings of Nietzsche. Translated and edited with commentaries by Walter Kaufmann. New York: The Modern Library, 1968. Includes (complete) *The Birth of Tragedy, The Case of Wagner, Beyond Good and Evil, On the Genealogy of Morals*, and *Ecce Homo*.

The Portable Nietzsche. Translated and edited by Walter Kaufmann. New York: Viking, 1954. Includes (complete) *Thus Spoke Zarathustra, Twilight of the Idols, The Antichrist, Nietzsche contra Wagner*.

Selections from Nietzsche's Works

A Nietzsche Reader. Edited and translated by R. J. Hollingdale. Harmondsworth: Penguin, 1977. A good selection of short snippets, organized by topic.

Nietzsche: Selections. Ed. Richard Schacht. New York: Macmillan, 1993. A good collection of excerpts from all of Nietzsche's works, published and unpublished, arranged chronologically. Particularly handy for some of the hard-to-get early essays—we have used these two extensively in the readings for the lectures.

Biographies and General Surveys

Ackermann, Robert John. *Nietzsche: A Frenzied Look.* Amherst: University of Massachusetts Press, 1990. (An offbeat but fascinating account of Nietzsche as continually obsessed with the Greeks.)

Chamberlain, Leslie. *Nietzsche in Turin.* New York: Picador, 1998. (A moving account of Nietzsche's last years.)

Clark, Maudemarie. *Nietzsche on Truth and Philosophy.* Cambridge: Cambridge University Press, 1990. (The best book on Nietzsche's general philosophical stance and his theory of knowledge.)

Danto, Arthur. *Nietzsche as Philosopher.* New York: Macmillan, 1965. (The first book to "translate" Nietzsche into the language of contemporary Anglo-American philosophy.)

Gilman, Sander L., ed. *Conversations with Nietzsche.* Trans. David Parent. New York: Oxford University Press, 1987. (Excerpts from letters and reminiscences.)

Hayman, Ronald. *Nietzsche: A Critical Life.* New York: Oxford University Press, 1980. (Perhaps the best single biography of Nietzsche, with an exaggerated sense of his impending madness.)

Heidegger, Martin. *Nietzsche.* 2 vols. Pfullingen: Neske, 1961. Trans. David Farrell Krell. 4 vols. New York: Harper and Row, 1979–86. (A book that has had tremendous influence on Nietzsche studies in Europe, dubiously interpreting Nietzsche as "the last metaphysician.")

Higgins, Kathleen Marie. *Nietzsche's Zarathustra.* Philadelphia: Temple University Press, 1987. (A sensitive and sympathetic reading of Nietzsche's most dramatic work as a work of literature as well as philosophy.)

Hollingdale, R. J. *Nietzsche*. London and New York: Routledge and Kegan Paul, 1973. (A good solid biography by one of Nietzsche's best translators.)

Hunt, Lester H. *Nietzsche and the Origin of Virtue*. London: Routledge, 1991. (An original interpretation of Nietzsche as a virtue ethicist and an "immoralist.")

Jaspers, Karl. *Nietzsche*, trans. Charles F. Wallraff and Frederick J. Schmitz. Tucson: University of Arizona Press, 1965. (A classic work, important for introducing Nietzsche to early twentieth century philosophy.)

Kaufmann, Walter. *Nietzsche: Philosopher, Psychologist, Antichrist*. 3rd ed., New York: Vintage, 1968. (The first ground-breaking work on Nietzsche in English, shattering the Nazi and German chauvinist myths and establishing Nietszsche as a respectable philosophical figure.)

Krell, David Farrell. *The Good European*. Chicago: University of Chicago Press, 1997. (A stunning collection of photographs and letters, tracing Nietzsche's wanderings through Southern Europe from his childhood and teaching in Basel to his last lonely years in northern Italy.)

Magnus, Bernd. With Jean-Pierre Mileur, Stanley Stewart. *Nietzsche's Case: Philosophy as/and Literature*. New York: Routledge, 1993. (A radical attempt to interpret Nietzsche in a postmodernist vein and understand his philosophical works as important works of literature.)

Nehamas, Alexander. *The Art of Living*. Cambridge: Cambridge University Press, 1998. (A study of Socrates' influence, with special attention to Nietzsche's admiration and use of him.)

———. *Nietzsche: Life as Literature*. Cambridge, MA: Harvard University Press, 1985. (One of the most elegant and influential attempts to interpret Nietzsche along postmodernist lines.)

Salomé, Lou. *Nietzsche*. Edited and translated by Siegfried Mandel. Redding Ridge, Connecticut: Black Swan Books, 1988. (One of the first Nietzsche studies, by the one woman who might have claimed to be Nietzsche's "true love.")

Schacht, Richard. *Nietzsche*. London: Routledge and Kegan Paul, 1983. (An outstanding comprehensive philosophical study.)

Solomon, Robert C. *From Hegel to Existentialism.* Oxford: Oxford University Press, 1988. (Studies in European philosophy, with several essays on Nietzsche.)

————, and Kathleen M. Higgins, *What Nietzsche Really Said.* New York: Random House, 1999. (An introduction to Nietzsche's thought, laying down the framework for the ideas in these lectures.)

Stern, J. P. *A Study of Nietzsche.* Cambridge: Cambridge University Press, 1979. (A good study of Nietzsche's life and works.)

Young, Julian. *Nietzsche's Philosophy of Art.* Cambridge: Cambridge University Press, 1992. (Special attention to Nietzsche's use of art to overcome pessimism and understand tragedy. Particularly good on Nietzsche's relation to Schopenhauer.)

Collections of Critical Essays on Nietzsche

Allison, David B., ed. *The New Nietzsche: Contemporary Styles of Interpretation.* New York: Dell, 1977. (Critical studies of Nietzsche, with emphasis on post-Heideggerian and new French interpretations.)

Krell, David Farrell, and David Wood, eds. *Exceedingly Nietzsche: Aspects of Contemporary Nietzsche Interpretation.* London: Routledge, 1988.

Magnus, Bernd, and Kathleen M. Higgins, *The Cambridge Companion to Nietzsche.* New York: Cambridge University Press, 1996. (Solid and wide-ranging critical studies of Nietzsche, with an emphasis on Nietzsche's influence on modern thought.)

Schacht, Richard, *Nietzsche, Genealogy, Morality.* Berkeley: University of California, 1997. (A variety of studies of Nietzsche's *On the Genealogy of Morals*, with numerous studies of genealogy, morality, and *ressentiment*.)

Sedgwick, Peter R., ed. *Nietzsche: A Critical Reader.* Oxford: Blackwell, 1995. (Critical studies of Nietzsche, with emphasis on recent French interpretations.)

Solomon, Robert C., ed. *Nietzsche: A Collection of Critical Essays.* New York: Doubleday, 1973. (More traditional critical studies of Nietzsche, with essays by Hermann Hesse, George Bernard Shaw, and Thomas Mann as well as more recent interpretations.)

————, and Kathleen M. Higgins, eds. *Reading Nietzsche.* New York: Oxford, 1988. (Studies of Nietzsche's individual works, with special attention to the approach to those works.

Notes